EXPANSION AND

AMERICAN INDIAN POLICY,

1783—1812

EXPANSION AND AMERICAN INDIAN POLICY, 1783—1812

By Reginald Horsman

University of Oklahoma Press
Norman and London

Copyright © 1967

Michigan State University Press

Library of Congress Catalog Card Number: 66-26958

Library of Congress Cataloging-in-Publication Data

Horsman, Reginald.
    Expansion and American Indian policy, 1783–1812 /
Reginald Horsman.
        p.   cm.
    Originally published: East Lansing : Michigan State Uni-
versity Press, 1967.
    Includes bibliographical references and index.
    ISBN 0-8061-2422-9 (pbk.)
    1. Indians of North America—Government relations—
1789–1869. 2. United States—Territorial expansion. 3. Indians. Treatment of—United States. I. Title.
E93.H79   1992
323.1'197—dc20   91-50858
                                                       CIP

Paperback edition published by arrangement with Michigan
State University Press by the University of Oklahoma Press,
Norman, Publishing Division of the University. Copyright
© 1967 by Michigan State University Press. All rights reserved.
Manufactured in the United States of America. First printing
of the Oklahoma Paperback, 1992.

2   3   4   5   6   7   8   9   10   11

Contents

Acknowledgment

I would like to thank the Graduate School of the University of Wisconsin for research support in the summer of 1962 and for grants-in-aid which have enabled me to complete the work for this book.

REGINALD HORSMAN

University of Wisconsin-Milwaukee

Preface to the University of Oklahoma Press Paperback Edition

IN THE TWENTY-FIVE YEARS since this book was first published, scholarly interest in the American Indian has blossomed. A host of books and articles have given new breadth and depth to Indian history. During this time there has been an attempt to shift the focus of attention away from familiar periods and topics to times and subjects previously neglected. As a result of these efforts, the mid-nineteenth and twentieth centuries have benefited from attention previously devoted to other periods. There has also been a significant and partially successful attempt to direct attention away from an emphasis on white attitudes and governmental policies to an emphasis on Indian cultures and the policies of the tribes themselves.

One result of these new interests has been a comparative neglect of some significant topics and significant eras; among them the shaping of governmental policy in the formative years of the new nation. This was a period of great expectations and bitter disappointments. Many of the first generation of American leaders, inspired by Enlightenment ideals, believed that the new United States was capable of achieving expansion with a good conscience. Viewing the American Indians from a position that was entirely ethnocentric, policy makers such as

Henry Knox and Thomas Jefferson hoped to acquire Indian lands by persuading the Indians that it was in their best interest to give up not only their lands but also their entire way of life. They did not believe that it was possible to share the lands east of the Mississippi River with Indian tribes, but they had hopes that some sharing might be possible with individual Indian farmers who had given up their own way of life.

These policies foundered on the compulsive land hunger of American frontiersmen, on the reality that most American leaders believed that expansion, not coexistence with the Indians, was vital for the future progress of the United States; and because most Indians were unwilling to give up all that they had known to meet the desires of the European invaders. The flowery rhetoric of Enlightenment idealism meant little or nothing to actual settlers, who often developed a hatred for Indians who fought to try to preserve their lands and their way of life. It became apparent early in the nineteenth century that even the presence of quite small groups of Indians, supposedly in the process of being transformed into American farmers, was not acceptable to frontiersmen, who wanted all, not some, of the land they were advancing over.

For leaders such as Henry Knox or Thomas Jefferson the problem was more complicated. While western settlers often had little or no compunction in killing or ousting the Indians who tried to resist the expansion of the transplanted Europeans, the early American leadership was concerned that the new republic should demonstrate the purity of its institutions and the nobleness of its intentions. In shaping his policies, Henry Knox wrote of his desire that the new nation should not be condemned by contemporary Europeans or by future historians. He wanted it to be known that this was no corrupt Spanish monarchy destroying the Indians of the New World, but a free republic providing hope to all the world's inhabitants.

In confronting the American Indians, most of the high hopes were in the process of disintegration by 1815. The American population grew and expanded with remarkable rapidity in the thirty years after the American Revolution. High ideals were swamped by the realities of providing protection and additional lands for the ever-increasing stream of settlers pouring into the Mississippi Valley. It is no surprise that American leaders were infinitely more responsive to the demands of their own electorate than to the complaints of Indians who saw boundary after boundary collapse under the relentless pressure of the westward advance.

The republican idealism that persuaded American leaders that Indians as well as settlers could be benefited by westward expansion also had shaped the governmental system that brought such hopes under constant attack. In the 1780s the Confederation Congress developed a policy that provided for the creation of new and equal states as pioneers advanced across the Mississippi Valley. The nature of the American territorial system and the rapidity of American expansion meant that regions which only recently had been fought over quickly became states. The senators and representatives who came to Congress from across the mountains generally viewed the Indians from the perspective of Indian warfare and the struggle for land, not from the perspective of the European Enlightenment.

The Europeans and their descendants who conquered the North American continent for the most part lacked any sense of cultural relativism. Even though many fur traders and some captives learned to appreciate a different way of life, the Europeans who went out to colonize lands around the world usually saw no value in the cultures they overran. The different ways of life that they discovered were not regarded as simply different, they were regarded as wrong. With this assumption dominating the thought of the Europeans, there was little chance of any satisfactory accord being reached with the inhabitants of the regions they were conquering.

This assumption of the superiority of the transplanted European culture dominated the thinking of the new American republicans as it dominated the thinking of Europeans throughout the world. Indeed, republican America took it a step further, for the leaders of the Revolutionary generation believed after their successful break from England that they were now offering a perfected version of European culture to the world.

Agreements with Indian tribes were made to be broken, because in the eyes of the "civilized" world the United States already had sovereignty over the lands westward to the Mississippi River; the only questions were how, when, and under what terms actual Indian dispossession would be arranged. For white negotiators, treaty language was merely a means of obtaining land with the least conflict and expense, and a means of deflecting Indian resistance until the next, inevitable cessions were necessary. For Indian negotiators, treaty language often represented solemn promises that they believed would be carried out.

Early American leaders wanted a good conscience when they shaped their Indian policies, they wanted policies that would reflect favorably on the ideals of the new republic, but above all else they wanted the land that they thought essential for the success of that republic. And ultimately the desire for land, not a desire for enlightened policies, shaped actions toward the Indians.

REGINALD HORSMAN

Milwaukee, Wisconsin

EXPANSION AND

AMERICAN INDIAN POLICY,

1783—1812

Establishing a Policy, 1783—1784

I

IN THE PRELIMINARY AGREEMENT for American independence which was signed by England and the United States in November 1782 there was no mention of the American Indians. Though they had been used extensively in the Revolution, it was not thought necessary to include them in the peace negotiations. This was no surprise. For the past century the Indians had served as pawns in a series of Anglo-French conflicts along the frontiers of North America, and in the Revolution they had again fallen between contending powers. For the most part they had cast their lot with the British for the simple reason that they had less to fear from British officials and traders than from American land speculators and farmers. The American victory in the Revolution was a disaster to the Indians. It meant that they were now left to face the Americans—who were angered by the Anglo-Indian Revolutionary alliance—with only such support as the British might be prepared to give them from Canada.

The territorial articles of the preliminary peace well illustrated the curious ambiguities of the American-Indian relationship. The American western boundary was placed on the Mississippi River and this boundary was confirmed by the definitive peace treaty signed at Paris on September 3, 1783. American settlement by no means reflected this western boundary. The first settlers had pushed doggedly through the Appalachian barrier and had begun the occupation of what are now the states of Kentucky and Tennessee, but for the most part the Americans were still confined to the area east of the Appalachians. Vermont, Maine, and western New York were still largely frontier areas. Western Pennsylvania had been opened to settlement in the decade preceding the Revolution, but Fort Pitt was still a frontier outpost in 1783. The back country of Virginia and the Carolinas was passing beyond the raw frontier stage as settlers pressed on into Kentucky and Tennessee, but Georgia was still largely unsettled.[1]

Yet, though the eastern half of the Mississippi Valley was for the most part unsettled by the Americans, it was no deserted wilderness. Its history is sometimes written as though settlers were to pour into a vast, empty valley but actually much of the eastern half of the Mississippi Valley was occupied by Indian tribes. Many of these tribes had fought successfully on the British side in the Revolution; others, on the banks of the Mississippi, hardly knew a revolution had taken place. Few of them could comprehend how the signing of a treaty in Paris between the English and the Americans could result in the transfer of their villages and hunting grounds to the new United States.

In March 1783 news of the preliminary articles of peace at last arrived in the United States, and immediate attention was given to the Indian problem. On April 11 Congress proclaimed the end of hostilities, and by the beginning of May steps had been taken to inform the Indians of peace and prepare them for treaties to end their participation in the conflict.[2] More important, and more difficult, was the task of formulating the policy on which these treaties would be based.

Though it might well be expected that the new United States would follow British and colonial precedents in acknowledging an Indian right of soil, the country for a time ignored this concept in seeking land in the Old Northwest. This stemmed both from a desire for revenge because of Indian hostility in the Revolution and from an over-optimistic belief in the degree to which the Indians would be overawed by the defeat of their British allies. To some extent this latter belief was understandable, for it was not expected in the spring of 1783 that the British would for twelve years retain control of the Northwest posts and encourage the Indians to resist American expansion.

In the years immediately following the Revolution the Americans assumed that they could secure Indian lands simply as a result of their victory over the British in the Revolution. In its desperate financial plight the United States saw its salvation in the sale to settlers and land companies of the western lands which in the 1780's were being ceded by the individual states to the federal government. By obtaining substantial cessions of lands from the Indians, the American government hoped to ease its financial plight and at the same time provide rich settlement areas for its citizens. The American government sadly underestimated the extent of Indian resistance.[3]

Within one week of the proclamation of the end of hostilities in April 1783, Revolutionary General Henry Knox wrote to George Washington and justified the retention of a military force on the grounds that it would be needed to protect the extensive western country ceded by the British to the Americans. If the western area was made secure, Knox argued, it would enable Congress to defray much of the expense arising from the war. Washington was in general agreement with Knox's plans and in June 1783 he supported another means of opening the western area to settlement. He urged that disbanded officers and men of the Continental Army should be given every encouragement to settle on the American frontiers. This would enable them to protect the frontiers, he argued, "and more than probably prevent the murder of many innocent families, which frequently, in their usual mode of extending our Settlements and Encroachments on the hunting grounds of the Natives, fall the hapless Victims to savage barbarity." Moreover, Washington stated, the appearance of so formidable a settlement in the vicinity of the Indian towns "would be the most likely means to enable us to purchase upon equitable terms of the Aborigines their right of preoccupancy; and to induce them to relinquish our Territories, and to remove into the illimitable regions of the West." Washington was presumably thinking of an Indian withdrawal beyond the Mississippi into Spanish territory.[4]

The contention of Knox and Washington that by the use of soldiers or ex-soldiers the Indians could be compelled to withdraw and the western lands opened to sale and settlement posed distinct problems to a nation that had frontiers from Maine to Georgia. It called for military forces far more powerful than the United States would or could afford in the years following the Revolution. Far more palatable was the advice of General Philip Schuyler of New York who wrote an exceedingly influential letter to the President of Congress at the end of July 1783. Schuyler's experience with Indian affairs in the Revolution gave weight to his suggestions and, though not all of them were immediately accepted, they served to modify the direct methods proposed by Knox and Washington.

Schuyler argued that it was not worthwhile to continue a war against the Indians. Even if the Indians were driven from the country, he asserted, they would return as soon as the force which expelled them had retired and the expense of such an endeavor would far exceed its value. If, on the other hand, they remained peacefully within the limits of the United States, this would not prevent the occupation of an extensive area between what the Americans now inhabited and what the Indians might be allowed to retain. Schuyler assumed that the American victory in the Revolution would force the Indians to make extensive cessions. Moreover, even the country which the Indians retained, argued Schuyler, could be taken whenever the United States so desired, "for as our settlements ap-

proach their country, they [the Indians] must, from the scar-
city of game, which that approach will induce to, retire farther
back, and dispose of their lands, unless they dwindle comparatively to nothing, as all savages have done, who gain their
sustenance by the chase, when compelled to live in the vicinity
of civilized people, and thus leave us the country without the
expense of a purchase, trifling as that will probably be." Indeed, argued Schuyler, if the Indians were allowed to remain
within United States territory, this would be an advantage for
if the Indians were driven into British territory, they would
add strength to Great Britain, harass the American frontiers
from a safe base, and deprive the United States of the fur
trade.[5]

Thus Schuyler was envisaging a much more sophisticated
policy than that of Knox and Washington. The Indians would
be forced to cede large areas as a result of their allegiance to
the British in the Revolution, but they could still live on
American territory further to the west. This in time would
also be yielded to the United States, for as the American settlers advanced to the borders of the Indian country, game and
Indians would diminish, and the remaining Indians, if any,
would for a small consideration make further cessions to the
Americans. Schuyler's letter was referred to a Congressional
committee which was attempting to formulate an Indian
policy, and with other papers on Indian affairs, the committee
later sent it to Washington for his comments.[6]

After reading these papers, Washington gave his own views
to the committee, through its chairman James Duane, on
September 7, 1783. He first stated that he completely agreed
with Schuyler's letter of July 29. Washington had presumably
been persuaded by Schuyler's letter to abandon his own idea
(expressed in June) of using force to persuade the Indians to
remove to "the illimitable regions of the West." Washington's
new suggestions reflected the ideas of Schuyler. The Indians
should first give up all their prisoners and be informed of the
cessions made to the United States by Great Britain in the
treaty of peace. They should then be told that, as they had

fought with the British in the Revolution, they could be compelled to retire with the British beyond the Great Lakes, but that the United States was prepared to be generous and allow them to stay. The United States would establish an American-Indian boundary line "beyond which we will *endeavor* to restrain our People from Hunting or Settling." "In establishing this line," Washington advised, "in the first instance, care should be taken neither to yield nor to grasp at too much." Moreover, compensation should be given if the Indians insisted or appeared dissatisfied, and a proclamation should be issued making it a felony for anyone to settle beyond the established line. In this way peace would be kept, American settlements would be compact, government would be well-established, a formidable barrier would be maintained, "and the Indians as has been observed in Gen Schuylers Letter will ever retreat as our Settlements advance upon them and they will be as ready to sell, as we are to buy; That is the cheapest as well as the least distressing way of dealing with them, none who are acquainted with the Nature of Indian warfare, and has ever been at the trouble of estimating the expence of one, and comparing it with the cost of purchasing their Lands, will hesitate to acknowledge."

Unless this policy were adopted, Washington suggested that the western country would be overrun by lawless adventurers ("Banditti"), and there was likely to be a renewal of Indian warfare. After warning the Congressional committee of the danger of placing too much power in the hands of Indian superintendents and of the necessity of trading fairly with the Indians, Washington went on to suggest the possible boundaries for American expansion across the Mississippi Valley. He envisaged an area of settlement bounded by Pennsylvania on the east, Lake Erie on the north, the Ohio River on the south, and a line running from the mouth of the Great Miami on the Ohio, up to the Mad River, north to the Maumee, and west to include Detroit. He thought this last inclusion necessary to prevent the British wooing away that area from American control. This cession would be large enough (it included most of the modern state of Ohio), he argued, and would prevent American efforts being dissipated in lawlessness over the whole western region. If it were not for the danger of leaving Detroit to British influence, Washington felt it might be better to have the line proceed along the Maumee to Lake Erie. In that case Detroit could become part of another state at a later date.

Though Washington was envisaging a definite line separating Indians and Americans, he did not regard this line as permanent in any way. The peroration of his letter returned to the ideas he had adopted from Philip Schuyler: "policy and œconomy point very strongly to the expediency of being upon good terms with the Indians, and the propriety of purchasing their Lands in preference to attempting to drive them by force of arms out of their Country; which as we have already experienced is like driving the Wild Beasts of the Forest which will return us [sic] soon as the pursuit is at an end and fall perhaps on those that are left there; when the gradual extension of our Settlements will as certainly cause the Savage as the Wolf to retire; both being beasts of prey tho' they differ in shape. In a word there is nothing to be obtained by an Indian War but the Soil they live on and this can be had by purchase at less expense, and without that bloodshed, and those distresses which helpless Women and Children are made partakers of in all kinds of disputes with them." [7]

Washington assumed that Schuyler's suggestions would produce expansion without war, but these arguments contained definite miscalculations. The initial error was the assumption that the Indians who had sided with the British in the Revolution would willingly make a large cession to the Americans and be grateful for what they were allowed to retain. The Indians were in fact still firmly in possession of the modern state of Ohio, and dislodging them was to prove an arduous task. The other fallacy in this reasoning was the hope that Indians wars could be avoided at each further cession in the westward progression of American-Indian boundaries. The concept of diminishing game and reduction in the number of Indians as the settlers advanced was true enough, but the theory of each successive area falling into American hands failed to allow for the desperate resistance put up at each boundary as the Indians realized that the game was disappearing and that their tribes were being demoralized. Schuyler and Washington failed to allow for the desperation of Indians faced with the loss of their traditional homes.

On September 22, 1783, Congress attempted to put into effect one segment of this policy when it agreed to issue a proclamation prohibiting settlement on lands inhabited or claimed by Indians outside the limits or jurisdiction of any state. The limitation was necessary because several of the states were showing great reluctance to allow federal government interference in what they considered their personal Indian relations. The Articles of Confederation, which had been put into effect in 1781, gave the federal government only power to negotiate with those Indians who were outside the jurisdiction of any state. This effort to prevent encroachment on Indian lands (which was combined with a prohibition of persons receiving gifts or cessions from the Indians without the permission of Congress) was to be frequently flouted—oftimes with the connivance or tacit approval of one or more of the individual states—but the federal government made an attempt to preserve the inviolability of its boundaries with the Indians. In this way it hoped to keep the peace until such time as the Indians would peacefully yield more lands.[8]

The report which was to guide American Indian policy until the last years of the Confederation was eventually adopted by Congress on October 15, 1783. The committee indicated at the beginning of the report that it had confined its remarks to Indian affairs in the northern and middle departments; because of insufficient information they left the area south of the Ohio for later action. The report, however, dealt at length with northern Indian affairs and showed throughout the extent to which the committee had been influenced by the suggestions of Schuyler and Washington. The report stated that it would be extremely difficult and expensive to try to expel the Indians and that even after that had been accomplished they would regain at least some of the land when the armies retreated. Moreover, even if they could be completely expelled, such action would strengthen the British in war and give them entire control of the fur trade in peace. Motives both of clemency and policy inclined the United States to grant the Indians peace, but it was both just and necessary "that lines of property should be ascertained and established between the United States and them, which will be convenient to the respective tribes, and commensurate to the public wants." This was necessary, argued the committee, because the United States was pledged to grant land as a bounty to its army (and could not afford to pay much for such lands), because the increase in population had made it necessary to make speedy provision for the extension of the territories of the United States, and because "the public creditors" had been led to believe (and had a right to expect) that these territories would be used to create a fund to extinguish the national debt.

The committee had thus decided that there should be peace, but that it should be a peace which would commence with an Indian land cession. This cession, it believed, was fully justified by the acts of aggression committed by the Indians during the war; the Indians themselves could not have "any reasonable objections." The Indians should make atonement, "and they possess no other means to do this act of justice than by a compliance with the proposed boundaries." The committee next quoted, almost directly, the words used by Washington in his letter to Chairman James Duane on September 7 when it stated that "care ought to be taken neither to yield nor require too much." It would be better to give some compensation for Indian claims rather than risk a war. The committee thought, however, that when the Indians had been told of the cost of the damages they had inflicted and what it had cost the United States to quell them, they would be inclined to suppress "extravagant demands."

After this remarkably optimistic preamble the committee presented a series of specific recommendations. A convention should be held with the Indians in the northern and middle departments, and they should be persuaded to give up their prisoners. Furthermore, they were to be informed that England had ceded all territory westward to the Mississippi. Then, still following Washington's recommendations, the committee stated that the Indians should be told that, as they had fought on the losing side with the British, they could be compelled to retire completely from American territory. However, as the United States was prepared to be generous, she would draw lines separating the Americans from the Indians. The committee used Washington's second suggestion for a western boundary line: from the mouth of the Great Miami, up to the Mad River, then to the Maumee, and along that river to Lake Erie. The committee also confirmed to the Oneidas and Tuscaroras (who had been friendly in the Revolution) the possession of their lands and suggested that a committee be appointed to draw up an ordinance for regulating the Indian trade.[9]

The philosophy which Congress had adopted to deal with the northwestern Indians ignored colonial experience, for it assumed that they could be dealt with as though they lacked even a right of soil in the land on which they lived. It made the mistake of assuming that the Indians would accept punishment (in the form of cession of lands) for fighting on the British side in the Revolution and ignored the consideration that, for the Indians, the Revolution had been only one episode in a long struggle of resistance to European farmers. Furthermore, the committee failed to indicate that the Indians had not even suffered heavy reverses in the land west of the Appalachians. Though the British had agreed in Paris to give the United States all the land westward to the Mississippi, this did not really reflect the military situation in the West. The victories of George Rogers Clark had been dissipated in the last years of the war, and the western Indians certainly had no reason to think that they had suffered any overwhelming military defeat. The Treaty of Paris did not reflect the realities of strength beyond the Ohio River.

By the time this October 1783 report had any practical effect in regard to the northwestern Indians, Congress had also accepted a report on southern Indian policy. This reflected not speed in producing the latter report, but considerable dilatoriness in using the former. The state of Indian affairs in the South was referred to a committee on October 16, 1783, but it was not until May 28, 1784, that Congress finally received its report. The committee first stated that many of the principles contained in the report of October 15, 1783, applied equally well to the southern department and that the committee proposed to adopt these principles to its use when circumstances were similar. The committee first optimistically and falsely reported that all claims made by South Carolina and Georgia upon the Indians had been satisfied and that "no subject of contention" threatened the United States in the southern department. The report did, however, concede that the quiet among the Indians might in some degree be the effect of disappointment and despair and expressed some doubt as to how long it might continue. Like the northern report, this one assumed that the Indians would have no "extravagant demands" and urged that all efforts should be made to preserve the peace.

The preliminary hopes were followed by the real business of the report: "Congress, however desirous they may be to gratify their better feelings in acts of humanity," stated the committee, "will not be warranted in advancing beyond the essential interests of their constituents; and furthermore generosity becomes bankrupt and frustrates its own designs by prodigal bounty." It seemed hardly likely that southern Indian policy would suffer from this latter defect. The gist of the matter was that the committee considered that the southern states, like the rest of the United States, were pledged to pay their public debts, to reward their own members of the army, and to provide for the settlement of an increasing population. Also, like the rest of the United States, they could afford to spend little to accomplish these ends. The committee thus thought that the Indians should "be prevailed upon . . . to make such cessions of uncultivated land to the States they inhabit respectively as may be convenient to those nations and commensurate to the present and approaching necessities of those States." As in the northern report it was suggested that the Indians could have no reasonable objections to these suggestions from the American government. It was recommended that conventions be held with the southern Indians to reiterate the points made to the northern Indians. In this report the boundary was left to the discretion of the commissioners, but special provision had to be made to counter the separate negotiations of southern states with the Indian tribes. The commissioners were instructed not to confirm in these new treaties any treaties previously concluded by an individual state unless such treaties were "perfectly consistent" with the philosophy now adopted.

This last suggestion emphasized the added complications which faced the southern negotiators. The rapacity of Georgia and North Carolina left little hope for subtlety in federal negotiations. Those states were eager for land and had less compunction than the federal government regarding the methods used to obtain it. Congress had indicated its desire to restrain the more obvious gaucheries of Georgia, but the report also indicated the weak position from which the central government approached its task of restraining the individual states and creating a unified Indian policy. It was suggested in the report that South Carolina furnish the commissioners with the goods and money they would need for these treaties and that these sums be credited against any unsatisfied requisitions of Congress from South Carolina. The task of centralizing Indian policy was made infinitely more difficult by the Confederation's lack of money. The last of the general suggestions made by the committee was one which was to become far more important in the next decade: the commissioners were urged to "use such arguments as shall appear to them most likely to prevail with the Indians to enter into the society of the Citizens of the United States." Little was to be done with this idea of civilization through the rest of the Confederation period, but it was to become an important issue of American policy under the new constitution.[10]

The Confederation Government was to find that obtaining land was nothing like the logical process described in these reports on northern and southern Indians. On one hand it was confronted with Indians who saw no reason to give reparation for their conduct in the Revolution, and on the other hand it was confronted with states which showed a marked reluctance to yield their sovereignty to the federal government. New York and Pennsylvania in the North and Georgia and North Carolina in the South had their own ideas about the formulation of Indian policy and they had little inclination to yield any powers that might injure their interests. Only as the central government obtained an unchallenged right to the lands of the Mississippi Valley could it hope to carry out an Indian policy unhampered by serious state interference, and in 1784 this time had not yet arrived. Even when the Mississippi Valley claims were yielded, the interference was not completely ended. Though New York had yielded her western claims in 1781, her interest in the fate of the Six Nations within her borders involved her in general Indian policy. Congress pressed hard to obtain state claims to western lands, but it was not until 1786 that she obtained an unfettered right to the land northwest of the Ohio. In the South it was an even longer process, for North Carolina made her final cession in 1789, and Georgia persisted in her claims until 1802.[11]

In the years immediately following the Revolution, the United States desperately needed peace with the Indians and possession of lands in the eastern Mississippi Valley. She hoped that the philosophy adopted in 1783-1784 would enable her to achieve both these ends, but was soon to discover that they were incompatible. Now she was to put herself in the position of making substantial demands without the force to support them. This was to bring difficulties in both the North and South and greatly increase the embarrassments of the Confederation Government.

The Policy in Practice, 1784—1786

II

THOUGH THE COMMITTEE on northwestern Indian affairs had urged upon Congress the need for prompt action, the Confederation Government proved incapable of operation. The report was presented on October 15, 1783, but it was not until March 4, 1784, that Congress finally elected five commissioners to negotiate with the northwestern Indians. Still there were further delays, for three of the original commissioners declined to accept appointment and the meeting planned for New York in April to determine procedure was delayed until August.[1]

Even before the commissioners gathered, their task had become more difficult. The first complication was that Congress had decided to try to obtain more land. In March 1784 a new committee (consisting of Thomas Jefferson, David Howell, and Hugh Williamson) had been appointed to revise the report of the previous October. As a result of its prompt revision, it was agreed to move the suggested boundary line further to the west. It was now to be drawn from the lowest point of the rapids of the Ohio (near modern Louisville) directly northward to the British-American boundary. The committee also suggested that in order to dissuade the Indians from ideas of a confederacy, negotiations should take place, when possible, with separate tribes rather than in one big conference as had been suggested in the previous October. This plan, however, was temporarily overthrown on April 16 when Congress decided that in the interest of speed and economy the commissioners should negotiate with the Indian tribes jointly.[2]

A more serious complication for the commissioners was the interference of the state of New York. Both New York and Pennsylvania were most interested in the proposed negotiation with the northwestern Indians, and New York had moved more rapidly than the federal government. As far back as March 1783 the New York Assembly had authorized the appointment of three commissioners for Indian affairs within the state, and for more than a year New York had been engaged in preliminary exchanges with the Six Nations. In April 1784 Governor George Clinton and the New York commissioners were given further authorization to enter into agreement with the Indians within the state, and the Six Nations were now invited to enter into a treaty.[3]

The Six Nations replied shrewdly to this offer. Joseph Brant, the well-educated, articulate Mohawk chief, attempted to draw the federal government into the negotiations. He accepted the idea of a treaty, suggested Fort Stanwix in the Mohawk Valley as a meeting place, and on July 21 informed the state of New York that the chiefs of other nations would accompany the Six Nations to Fort Stanwix. He particularly asked New York, however, to acquaint Congress of these plans so that all the states could send representatives for a general settlement with the Six Nations.[4]

In the meantime the United States Commissioners were tagging along well behind the state of New York. On August 10 two of them—Richard Butler and Arthur Lee—wrote to Governor Clinton and asked what steps New York had taken to raise her quota of troops for protecting the commissioners at the coming United States treaty. Clinton replied that he could not raise regular troops because the New York Assembly was not in session, but that if necessary he would raise a force from the militia. He then officially informed the United States Commissioners of New York's plans for a separate treaty. He was completely blunt in his assertion of the rights of New York and in his rejection of Congressional interference. He told the United States Commissioners that the Six Nations had informed him that they would be accompanied to Fort Stanwix by deputies of other nations "possessing the territory within the Jurisdiction of the United States. I shall have no objection to your improving this incident to the advantage of the United States, expecting however and positively stipulating that no long agreement be entered into with Indians residing within the Jurisdiction of this State, with whom only I mean to treat, prejudicial to its rights." [5]

Governor Clinton having already arranged the time and place of the treaty, the United States Commissioners could do little but attend. They informed Clinton, most unhappily, that as the Indians were already committed to attend at Fort Stanwix, they would meet with them there in September, but they pointedly praised the conduct of the Pennsylvania commissioners who had agreed to subordinate their business to the general treaty. Such was the inauspicious beginning of post-Revolutionary Congressional Indian policy. [6]

The New York commissioners met with the Indians from August 31 to September 10 and accomplished nothing. They requested a cession of land within the state of New York, but generally acted more mildly than had been recommended as a federal policy in the Congressional report of October 1783. The Indian delegates informed the commissioners that at present they had no powers from their tribes to cede lands, and this was accepted by the New York representatives. At the unsuccessful conclusion of New York's negotiatons two representatives remained to observe the Congressional proceedings and attempt to impede any action detrimental to the interests of the state of New York.[7]

Congressional negotiations with the Six Nations finally began on October 12, and the commissioners compensated for their loss of face to New York by being particularly domineering in regard to the Six Nations. They pointed out the extent of British cessions and stressed that in the peace treaty the British had completely ignored the Indians. The Indians spoke for an Ohio River boundary, but they were soon overridden by the American commissioners. On October 20 the pretence of parleying was brought to an end when the Six Nations were informed of the treaty they would have to sign. Furthermore, they were told that they were at the mercy of the United States: "You are mistaken in supposing that having been excluded from the United States and the King of Great Britain, you are become a free and independent nation, and may make what terms you please. It is not so. You are a subdued people; you have been overcome in war which you entered into with us, not only without provocation, but in violation of most sacred obligations."

The American commissioners then told the Indians the boundaries they would be given. Though the Oneida and Tuscarora, who had been friendly to the United States in the Revolution, were confirmed in the possession of their lands, the Six Nations as a whole were forced to yield all their claims to land west of the western boundary of Pennsylvania. The Six Nations were told that more land had been left to them than they could have expected from their conduct in the Revolution: "The King of Great Britain ceded to the United States *the whole,* by the right of conquest they might *claim the whole.* Yet they have taken but a small part, compared with their numbers and their wants. Their warriors must be provided for. Compensation must be made for the blood and treasures which they have expended in the war. The great increase of their people, renders more lands essential to their subsistence. It is therefore necessary that such a boundary line should be settled, as will make effectual provisions for these demands, and prevent any future cause of difference and dispute." On October 22 the Treaty of Fort Stanwix was signed. The United States had obtained the rather nebulous claims of the Six Nations to the Ohio Valley, and the commissioners had made it clear that they were quite prepared to dictate treaties to the Indians.[8]

After the successful conclusion of the Treaty of Fort Stanwix, two of the commissioners—Arthur Lee and Richard Butler—travelled west to meet with Indians from beyond the Ohio who had not attended the Fort Stanwix meeting. The commissioners arrived at Fort Pitt early in December and eventually met with the Indians at Fort McIntosh, some thirty miles down the river, in January 1785. Present at the treaty were the Wyandots, Delawares, Ottawas, and Chippewas; the Shawnees were conspicuous by their absence. The commissioners followed the formula which had been used with at least temporary success at Fort Stanwix, for they told the Indians of the British cessions, that the Indians had been ignored in the peace treaty, and that the Six Nations had already been "allotted" land to live and hunt upon. The Indians, as at Fort Stanwix, stated their own claims, but they were brushed aside by the commissioners in a particularly blunt statement of the American position: "You next express your gladness that the Six Nations your uncles have *given us* a part of *their* country. But it is quite the contrary. We have given the hostile part of the Six Nations some of the country which we have conquered from them." The details of Indian claims and titles, stated the commissioners, might be of interest to the Indians, "But to us & to the business of the Council Fire to which we have called you, they have no relation; because we claim the country by conquest; and are to *give* not to receive." As at Fort Stanwix, the commissioners dictated the terms of a settlement. The treaty which was signed on January 21 enclosed the signatory tribes (the Wyandot, Delaware, Chippewa, and Ottawa) within an area bounded by the Cuyahoga River on the east, a line from just above Fort Laurens to the west branch of the

Great Miami on the south, the St. Mary's and the Maumee on the west, and Lake Erie on the north. These tribes yielded what is now eastern and southern Ohio to the United States.[9]

There was one significant omission in this pattern of cession —the Shawnee had not yet signed away lands to the north of the Ohio, and they were one of the strongest tribes in the region. In February 1785 a Congressional committee was appointed to consider the Treaty of Fort McIntosh. It reported that in order to give greater security to the frontier settlements it would be necessary to hold a treaty conference even further to the west, not only with the Shawnee but also with the tribes along the Wabash. But once again Congressional dilatoriness delayed proceedings. Though Congress decided in March 1785 that further negotiations were needed in the Old Northwest, it was not until June that the details were worked out. The commissioners were enjoined to follow the October 1783 report, except that Congress now repealed the part of that report which delineated the boundary and urged the commissioners to make the cession as liberal and extensive as possible.[10]

In July and August 1785 the commissioners sent messages to the western Indians asking them to assemble in the fall.[11] There was every sign that an agreement would be difficult to accomplish, for the Indians were recovering from the shock of their desertion by the British at the end of the Revolution, and resentment was growing against the dictated treaties of Fort Stanwix and Fort McIntosh. It was quite obvious that however overcome the Indians had been at the treaty negotiations, they were not going to acquiesce in the notion that all the land to the Mississippi was for the Americans to dispose of as they wished. The Indian dissatisfaction was increased by the attitude of the British in Canada. In spite of the peace treaty the British had retained control of the line of posts, including Detroit, south of the Great Lakes, and they assured the Indians that they had not intended to give the Americans absolute right to all Indian lands westward to the Mississippi.[12]

The United States assumed an attitude towards the Indians during this period which ill-reflected actual American power. The victory over England had bred an over-confidence which was to be expiated in a ten-year struggle for the land of the Old Northwest. At a time when the United States had neither the money nor the army to undertake extensive operations against the Indians, her envoys talked and acted as though the least Indian resistance would be countered by an overwhelming display of force. For a time the Indians were apparently mesmerized by this bluff and the very audacity of the American statements, but they soon woke up.

The hope of obtaining a treaty of cession from all the tribes which might possibly resist the American advance across the Ohio faded in the fall of 1785. Signs of Indian resistance were increasing daily, and it seemed obvious that there would be a poor attendance at the proposed treaty conference.[13] This eventually took place at the mouth of the Great Miami on the Ohio River in January 1786. Apart from some Wyandots and Delawares who renewed the Treaty of Fort McIntosh, the only tribe to attend was the Shawnee. Negotiations followed the pattern already laid down at Fort Stanwix and Fort McIntosh, for the terms of the treaty were dictated by the American commissioners, and only a slight modification of the boundary was allowed when the Shawnee chiefs protested that they were being left no land to live or raise corn upon. "God gave us this country," argued one Shawnee chief, "we do not understand measuring out the lands, it is all ours." The commissioners replied that the Shawnee had fought against the Americans in the Revolution and that the British had given the Shawnee lands to the United States. "We plainly tell you," stated Commissioner Richard Butler, "that this country belongs to the United States—their blood hath defended it, and will forever protect it. Their proposals are liberal and just; and you instead of acting as you have done, and instead of persisting in your folly, should be thankful for the forgiveness and offers of kindness of the United States." For the time being the Shawnee resistance collapsed, and the chief who had fiercely defended the Indian right to the land in the morning stated in the afternoon, "Brethren, our people are sensible of the truths you have told them. You have everything in your power—you are great, and we see you own all the country." The treaty was then signed and the Shawnee were "allotted" lands on which to live west of the Great Miami.[14]

By the end of January 1786 the American government had dictated to the Indians of the Old Northwest three treaties, all of which were based on the philosophy that the land to the Mississippi was American by right of conquest and that the United States could automatically draw boundary lines which would allow for American expansion. The signatory tribes had by then yielded what is now eastern and southern Ohio. However, the Indians resented the manner in which these negotiations had been conducted and resented even more the movement of settlers across the Ohio. Their determination to overthrow the dictated treaties was strengthened by British reluctance to consummate the Northwest cession made at Paris in 1783. The British still refused to withdraw from the Northwest posts and encouraged the Indians to resist the American frontier advance. In 1786 Indian depredations increased along the Northwest frontier causing great consternation in Congress, for the state of Confederation finances would not permit adequate frontier defense. Accordingly, Congress vacillated, and some members argued that the extent of the attacks was being exaggerated. Virginia showed more energy, though, for it was her frontier settlement of Kentucky that was being attacked. In October 1786 Colonel Benjamin Logan raided Shawnee towns on the Great Miami, but George Rogers Clark was forced to turn back before he had succeeded in attacking Wabash towns. These expeditions, not strong enough to overawe the frontier tribes, only increased the probability of outright Indian war.[15]

In November and December 1786 a general council of Indian tribes was held at the mouth of the Detroit River. The council objected to the treaties signed since 1783 on the grounds that they had been signed by individual tribes, and the theory was put forward that land cessions would be valid only if agreed to by the whole confederacy that was forming in the Northwest. The confederacy suggested a treaty meeting in the spring (though the message had not even reached Congress by spring) and requested that in the meantime surveyors and settlers not cross the Ohio River. The Northwest tribes were still hoping to block American settlement at the Ohio River.[16]

By the end of 1786 American plans for expansion across the Ohio into the Old Northwest were encountering ever increasing difficulty. The Indians, still resentful of the manner in which they had been forced to sign treaties after 1783, were engaged in open hostilities. Though the United States had promised to meet any such resistance by driving the Indians out of American territory, the country was so beset by financial problems and weakened by internal bickering that she was in no position to enforce her threats. As Indian resistance strengthened, Congress began to consider how its policy could be changed to permit peaceful American advance northwest of the Ohio.

American Indian policy south of the Ohio in the years after 1783 was hindered by the same problems as in the North: the dilatoriness of Congress, a shortage of money, and the interference of individual states. The last of these problems was an especially decisive factor in the South, for, as North Carolina did not make a final cession of her Mississippi Valley land claims until 1789, and Georgia not until 1802, federal government Indian policy was of vague legality in the southern half of the Mississippi Valley. Georgia and North Carolina felt free to pursue their objects with little regard for Congressional opinion and looked upon the efforts of Congress to negotiate with the Indians as an interference with their rights as sovereign states. An additional complication stemmed from the efforts of the semi-independent state of Franklin. This trans-Appalachian body was attempting to break away from the control of North Carolina and hoped to receive Congressional recognition as a full-fledged member of the Confederation. Meanwhile, Franklin pursued an aggressive land policy and aroused intense opposition among the Cherokees. As these various pressures were exerted on the Indians of the Southwest, they increasingly turned toward Spain, who was quite willing to use them as a means of perpetuating her own interests in the lower Mississippi valley.[17]

Congress was extraordinarily slow in negotiating with the southern tribes. The report on southern Indian affairs was eventually received by Congress on May 28, 1784, and most southerners interested in peace with the Indian tribes considered it essential that action be taken on the report before the adjournment of Congress at the beginning of June. When, on June 3, an attempt was made to delay adjournment for consideration of the report on southern Indian affairs, the effort failed owing to the objection of Massachusetts, Connecticut, New York, and New Jersey. The northeastern states were not prepared to continue the session to consider southern Indian relations, and, as a result, any possible action on the report was put off until Congress met again at the end of the year.[18]

In December Congress again procrastinated by appointing yet another committee, a committee to consider the report which had been presented in May.[19] This latest committee finally presented its report on March 4, 1785, recommending that commissioners should be immediately appointed to negotiate with the southern Indians and reiterating the familiar arguments that white prisoners in Indian hands were to be given up, the Indians were to be told of the cessions made by Great Britain and of the mercy of the United States. But at least in one regard these recommendations differed from those for the North, for the commissioners were enjoined to discover the true limits of lands purchased by authorized persons in southern states, and the boundary line was to be run accordingly. Moreover, the commissioners were to inform the governors of the four southern states of the time and place of their treaty convention so that representatives could be sent to explain the extent of previous purchases. The Indians were to be told that white settlers would be dissuaded from settling on the Indian side of the line, and it was suggested that the Indians be given the power to expel settlers who did not retire six months after being warned. It was also suggested that agents be appointed to reside among the Indians to discover their needs and protect them from fraud. Once again, as in the previous May, it was suggested that South Carolina should, for the time being, provide the money required for carrying out the treaty.[20]

This report of March 4 was recommitted on the 10th and the committee presented a revised report on the following day. This report made some interesting omissions from the original. The commissioners were no longer directed to ascertain the limits of lands previously purchased from the Indians in order to draw the boundary, and though the southern governors were still to be informed of the time and place of the treaty meeting, so that they could send representatives, nothing was said of these representatives explaining the extent of previous purchases. However, the report also omitted that clause which had suggested that the Indians be given the power to expel settlers who had not moved after six months warning. The decision to give no formal recognition to previous purchases was destined to meet with considerable opposition in the South, and the weakness of the Confederation was well demonstrated when the revised report spelled out in even more detail the extent to which the Congressional Commissioners would depend on southern support. The commissioners were to be empowered to apply to the "supreme executives" of Virginia, North Carolina, South Carolina, or Georgia for one hundred and fifty or less militia to protect them at the treaty conference and to the same states for financial support. Such support was to be applied against the Confederation requisitions for 1786.[21]

Congress debated this revised report for several days before finally reaching agreement. Maryland and Rhode Island (states which possessed no claims to western land) unsuccessfully attempted to strike out that clause which said the governors of the southern states should be informed of the time and place of the treaty, and eventually, on March 15, 1785, the report was accepted. It was now stated specifically that the commissioners could use up to nine thousand dollars for the expenses of the treaty and up to four thousand dollars for presents to the Indians. Finally, on the last day of March, two years after Congress had received news of the signing of the preliminary articles of peace, five commissioners were appointed to negotiate with the southern Indians.[22]

These commissioners were given a formidable task. From the Congressional point of view it was essential that peace on the southern frontier should, for the moment, take precedence over expansion. Congress would be content with peace and the *status quo* in the South if this could be accompanied by Indian cessions northwest of the Ohio. These Congressional views did not accord with the ideas of North Carolina, Franklin, or Georgia. Residents of these areas were anxious to clear Indian titles from lands they wanted to settle, and they were not fastidious in the methods used to accomplish this. Georgia in particular looked upon herself as a beleaguered outpost. To encourage immigration and expansion in that sparsely populated state, it was thought essential to push the Indians westwards. Moreover, land speculators encouraged the state government to press a vigorous Indian policy.[23]

Several treaties already complicated the task of the commissioners by the time they proceeded south to negotiate with the Indians. In May 1783 Georgia had obtained a tract of land between the Tugalo and Apalachee rivers from the Cherokee, then discovered it was Creek land and in November of the same year obtained a cession of the same land from a few conveniently available Creeks. The Treaty of Augusta was considered invalid by most of the Creeks and by their skillful leader Alexander McGillivray, but Georgia persisted in acting as though the treaty had been signed with the perfect consent of the whole Creek nation. Georgia's persistence helped to drive the Creeks into the eagerly awaiting arms of the Spaniards, and at Pensacola in the spring and summer of 1784 the Spaniards reached agreements, not only with the Creeks, but

27

also with the Chickasaws and the Choctaws. These tribes placed themselves under the general protection of the Spanish and prepared to resist the importunities of the Georgia settlers and land speculators. By the time the Congressional Commissioners were appointed in 1785, Georgia had decided that the land obtained at the Treaty of Augusta was insufficient, and she was hopeful of persuading some of the more complaisant Creeks to yield further lands before Congress interfered in southern Indian affairs.[24]

North Carolina showed even less regard for Indian rights and in May 1783 confiscated all Indian lands within the State except Cherokee lands between the French Broad and Tennessee Rivers. This simple confiscation was easier to proclaim than carry out, and it was received with anguished outcries and bitter resistance from Cherokees and Chickasaws as settlers advanced on to their lands. North Carolina land speculators increased the confusion by entering into separate negotiations for desirable land, and from 1784 the proposed state of Franklin added her grasping policies to the chaos of southern Indian affairs. In June 1785 at the Treaty of Dumplin Creek, Franklin persuaded the Cherokees to make large cessions south of the French Broad and Holston Rivers. (This at a time when the Cherokee were already incensed by continued pressure.) [25]

In the Old Northwest in these years the Congressional Commissioners assumed a domineering attitude and dictated treaties of cession to the stunned Indian tribes. In the Southwest the commissioners were faced with the task of restraining over-eager southern states, appeasing the resentful Indians, and making possible the peaceful sale and settlement of the land northwest of the Ohio. These southern commissioners had only limited success.

The United States Commissioners determined to negotiate with the Creeks at Galphinton on the Ogeechee River in the fall of 1785. This plan proved a failure, for the main body of the Creek nation did not arrive at the meeting place, and the commissioners thought it futile to treat with those Creek chiefs who did arrive.[26] Accordingly, early in November the United States Commissioners left Galphinton and proceeded to Hopewell on the Keowee River to negotiate with the other southern tribes. The Georgia commissioners were less perturbed than those of the United States by the lack of influential Creeks at Galphinton. As soon as the United States Commissioners departed, Georgia concluded a treaty with the Creeks who were present. This treaty confirmed the Treaty of Augusta and gave Georgia even more land by drawing a boundary from the forks of the Oconee and Ocmulgee Rivers south to the source of the St. Mary's. Thus Georgia compounded her previous actions by signing another treaty with a far from adequate representation of the Creek nation.[27]

At Hopewell the United States Commissioners were more fortunate than at Galphinton, yet once again their policy failed to win the support of the southern states. On November 28, 1785, the commissioners signed the Treaty of Hopewell with a good representation of Cherokees. This treaty attempted to establish friendship between Congress and the Cherokees, and the boundary that was drawn was a moderate one—so moderate in fact that it infuriated the state of North Carolina and its representative at the negotiations, William Blount. Though the Cherokees acknowledged that certain lands in North Carolina west of the Blue Ridge were American and conceded a tract south of the Cumberland River, in what are now the states of Tennessee and Kentucky, the line gave much less to the Americans than North Carolina wanted. Instead, settlers were left on the Indian side of the boundary line, and the Treaty of Dumplin Creek signed in June 1785 by the state of Franklin was repudiated by the American commissioners. William Blount immediately protested that the treaty violated the rights of North Carolina, and Congress found it impossible to enforce rigorously the boundaries that had been agreed upon.[28]

The commissioners remained at Hopewell after the treaty with the Cherokees, and in January 1786 succeeded in signing treaties with the Choctaws and the Chickasaws. In both of these treaties the commissioners attempted to keep the peace and thwart the more extravagant claims of settlers and land speculators by drawing boundary lines which reflected the situation immediately before the signing of the preliminary articles of peace with the British in November 1782. William Blount protested the treaty with the Chickasaws as he had that with the Cherokees, and these negotiations ended on the same sour note with which they had begun at Galphinton in October 1785.[29] In April 1786 North Carolina tried to persuade Congress to disavow the treaties with the Cherokees and the Chickasaws in so far as they allotted these Indians hunting grounds within the State without her permission. This attempt failed.[30]

Relations with the southern Indians were left in a most confused and precarious state by these treaties of late 1785 and early 1786. Georgia and North Carolina did not agree with them and were obviously quite prepared to thwart the intentions of the federal government. The Creeks had shunned the negotiations at Galphinton and McGillivray was quite capable of playing off the Spanish against the Americans in order to bolster the position of his tribe. Considerable forbearance and skill were needed in the South if Indian war was to be avoided, but the year 1786 brought neither.

Georgia continued to pressure the Creeks for land and in November 1786 received another confirmation of land gains of the 1780's when she signed the Treaty of Shoulderbone with the usual contingent of tame Creeks. Before that unfortunate treaty had been accomplished, the state of Franklin had already done its own part to bring Indian war to the South by signing the Treaty of Chota Ford with the Cherokees in July 1786. Both of these treaties secured additional land cessions from the Indians, but at the cost of driving them to desperation. Incidents and minor hostilities increased in the summer of 1786, and there seemed little that could be called a coherent policy in the whole southern region.[31]

The year 1786 thus brought a breakdown of policy in both the North and South. In the North the treaties of the 1784-

1786 period had nominally secured most of what is now the state of Ohio, but these treaties had been dictated to unwilling tribes who by 1786 were awakening from the shock of their desertion by the British in the Revolution. Now, encouraged by the British and at first by the leadership of the Mohawk Joseph Brant, these northwestern tribes were preparing to resist the contention that all the land to the Mississippi was American. They were already raiding the American frontier and desultory skirmishes would soon turn into all out Indian war if no solution could be found. In the South the federal government had played only an insignificant part in the years from the Revolution to 1786. The treaties that had been signed had been attempts to appease Indians maddened by the ruthlessness of southern frontier expansion more than the beginning of a positive and coherent national policy. The United States wanted to establish boundary lines and keep the peace in the South, while using the area northwest of the Ohio to ease America's financial problems and provide room for expansion. But by 1786 both of these objects were failing. The southern Indians had been driven to the verge of outright war by the pressures of southern expansion. The northern tribes were demanding that settlers and surveyors should not cross the Ohio and that the treaties of the postwar period should be re-negotiated. Faced by disaster, the United States began in 1786 and 1787 to change its methods. The overt expansionism of the immediate postwar period had failed, and some new policy had to be evolved.

A New Start, 1786—1789

III

ONGRESS'S FIRST REACTION to the treaties signed in January 1786 was that its policies had been successful. On May 17, 1786, the committee to which these treaties had been referred reported that it was no longer necessary to keep active the commissions for treating with the Indians. The committee argued that the commissions had fulfilled the task for which they had been created and any future relationship with the Indian tribes could be maintained less expensively by an organized Indian department. As a result of this report the commissions were brought to an end in July 1786.[1]

In spite of the assertions of the committee, it was becoming increasingly obvious that the commissioners had not fulfilled the objectives of peaceful expansion. In June 1786 Henry Knox, who had been appointed Secretary at War in the spring of the previous year, reported that in his opinion the troops now in service were "utterly incompetent" to protect the frontier of the Old Northwest from the incursions of the Indian tribes. If a general war occurred, the American army would have to be increased and new posts established deep in the Indian country.[2] The thought of this additional expense was a sobering one to the members of Congress, and they readily pressed ahead with a new measure which they optimistically hoped would help obviate the threat of war.

This measure was an ordinance for the creation of an Indian department. It was first reported out of committee on June 28 and eventually enacted by Congress on August 7, 1786. The report was vigorously debated, and some of the southern states showed marked reluctance to give any additional power over Indian affairs to the central government. By the ordinance the Indian department was divided into districts north and south of the Ohio River; each district was to have a superintendent responsible to the Secretary at War. In the report as it came from committee there were various details regarding the political activities of the superintendents, but as eventually enacted the ordinance was more concerned with matters of trade. Only United States citizens were to be allowed to reside or trade among the Indians, and even they would need a license. Georgia and North Carolina made determined efforts to place in the ordinance a provision which would guarantee noninterference with the rights of any state within its own limits, but in the end they were obliged to accept a somewhat watered-down clause which stated that where transactions with the Indians could not be carried out without interference with the legislative rights of a state, the superintendent would act in conjunction with the authorities of that state.[3]

Though this ordinance represented the desire of the central government to impose its control upon Indian affairs and bring to an end the emergency conditions of the postwar period, it had little immediate effect. The late summer and fall of 1786 were filled with reports of the dangers of Indian war. In September Colonel Benjamin Logan attacked Shawnee towns on the Great Miami, and at the end of the year the northern Indians met to present their demands for a re-negotiation of the treaties of the postwar period. It was quite obvious that a confederacy was developing to resist American expansion into the Old Northwest.[4]

In the South not only were the Indians displeased, Georgia and North Carolina were objecting bitterly to Congressional policy. On October 20 the Congressional committee which had been appointed to consider the warnings of the Secretary at War reported that there was great danger of a general war which would include both northern and southern Indians and which "will be attended with the most dangerous and lasting Consequences." The committee recommended an increase in the army, not only to protect the frontiers, but also to provide for the settlement of lands "which have been so much relied on" for the payment of American debts. In accordance with these resolutions Congress agreed to increase the army from seven hundred to over two thousand men, and the Board of Treasury was directed to devise ways and means of paying for the support of these troops.[5]

Ten days later, on October 30, 1786, another report on Indian affairs was presented to Congress; this report demonstrated not only disgust at the present Indian policy but also at the whole operation of the Confederation Government. This committee had members from Virginia, Maryland, South Carolina, Massachusetts, and Pennsylvania and had been set up to consider complaints regarding Virginia's military actions against the Indians, as well as general reports on the dangers of Indian war. It was also supposed to deal with the complaints of Georgia and North Carolina regarding federal Indian policy, but it left this question to the superintendent of Indian affairs for the southern department. The report was written in the hand of Henry Lee of Virginia, and it baldly asserted that "the offensive operations commenced by the inhabitants of Kentucky are authorized by self preservation and their experience of the imbecility of the fœderal government." The committee was convinced of the hostile disposition of the Indians. It thought that this arose from their lack of respect for the abilities of the United States Government and that this in turn stemmed from the manner in which Great Britain had retained control of the northwestern posts.[6]

The easy confidence that the Indians would yield lands as compensation for their actions in the war had been severely shaken by the end of 1786. In December John Jay wrote to Thomas Jefferson that he thought Indian affairs had been ill-managed; Indians had been murdered and the tribes were angered by the avidity with which the Americans had sought to acquire their lands. "Would it not be wiser," wrote Jay, "gradually to extend our Settlements, as want of Room should make it necessary." He feared that the scattering of settlers throughout the wilderness would people it with white savages in place of the present "tawny ones." [7] This cry of gradual expansion had long been uttered, but it was apt to be drowned by the clamor of western settlers and land speculators. It also stirred the protests of those Indians who looked upon every cession, gradual or not, as the loss of homes and hunting grounds.

Faced by the imminent danger of general war and by an empty treasury, Congress began to retreat from its high-handed attitude of the immediate postwar period. On February 20, 1787, a committee reported on instructions proposed by the Secretary at War for the superintendents of Indian affairs. The instructions accepted by the committee stated that "Most important considerations render it necessary that the United States should be at peace with the Indians, provided it can be obtained and preserved consistently with the justice and dignity of the nation." Peace indeed was a necessity for the Confederation, and perhaps with an eye to the southern states the committee asserted that "the United States are fixed in their determination, that justice and public faith shall be the basis of all their transactions with the Indians." The superintendents were instructed to cultivate both trade with the tribes and the friendship of the chiefs. Yet, in spite of talk of friendship, the committee feared war, and the superintendent of the northern district was instructed to discover, as soon as possible, the real designs of the Indians.[8] Congress, in truth, was in a desperate plight. Henry Knox declared at the beginning of March: "The treasury has been declining daily for these last two years—if it is not in the last gasp I am mistaken." This situation was nakedly revealed when Congress was obliged to disband most of the troops that had been authorized by the resolution of the previous October.[9] The Confederation Congress simply did not have the means to carry out a forceful policy.

Finally in a report to Congress on July 10, 1787, Secretary at War Henry Knox stated flatly what had been often suggested during the previous year. He first said that the frontiers of Virginia bordering on the Ohio were under attack and that he believed that the Indians and whites would never be good neighbors: "The one side anxiously defend their lands which the other avariciously claim. . . . Either one or the other party must remove to a greater distance, or Government must keep them both in awe by a strong hand, and compel them to be moderate and just." Knox went on to say that to carry out this policy the United States would need fifteen hundred troops rather than the five hundred which were now in the West. He even went so far as to outline how he would use them, but ended by acknowledging that "the depressed state of the finances will not admit of the measure." Thus the present troops would have to be disposed as effectively as possible, and a new treaty negotiated with the Shawnees and the tribes on the Wabash. If this did not succeed, then what there was of a regular army, with the addition of militia, should attack the Indian towns. But Knox once again capped his plans with the assertion that "in the present embarrassed state of public affairs and entire deficiency of funds an indian war of any considerable extent and duration would most exceedingly distress the United States." The entire report was a depressing one. Knox acknowledged that it was difficult to judge whether whites or Indians were in the wrong, that negotiation should be tried, but that war might be necessary and this would be disastrous to the United States.[10]

Though the majority agreed that the Indians were on the brink of a general war which would be disastrous to the Confederation Government, there was no question of Congress receding from its basic objectives. Western land was still looked upon as an essential source of revenue, and land had to be provided for those who wished to move northwest of the Ohio. Though some expressed the opinion that western expansion would only weaken the eastern states, Congress, in the famous Northwest Ordinance of July 1787, committed itself quite openly to expansion across the Old Northwest. The United States had in the period from 1781 secured from the individual states the most important claims to the land of the Old Northwest. She had secured them with the promise that this area would ultimately be formed into separate states which would enter the Union on a basis of equality with the older states. This ordinance of July 1787 provided a plan for the settlement of the Old Northwest and superseded the earlier Jefferson plan, which had been passed as a resolution of Congress on April 23, 1784.[11]

The Northwest Ordinance made it quite clear that, whatever was said to the Indians and however strong the fears of war, the United States intended to settle the area from the Ohio to the Mississippi River. The beginning of Article IV stated that "the said territory, and the States which may be formed therein, shall remain forever a part of this Confederacy of the United States of America," and Article V outlined the bounds of the states to be established in the Old Northwest. There were to be not less than three nor more than five states in an area bounded by Pennsylvania on the east, the American-Canadian boundary on the north, the Ohio River on the south, and the Mississippi on the west. After these territorial plans, which were in direct opposition to the Indian idea that American settlement should stop at the Ohio River, the phrases on Indian relations expressed in Article III become meaningless: "The utmost good faith shall always be observed towards the Indians; their land and property shall never be taken from them without their consent; and in their property, rights and liberty, they shall never be invaded or disturbed, unless in just and lawful wars authorised by Congress; but laws founded in justice and humanity shall from time to time be made, for preventing wrongs being done to them, and for preserving peace and friendship with them." It was hardly likely that the American and Indian concepts of "just and lawful wars" would be identical.[12]

Only a week after Knox had presented his depressing report on frontier conditions, the message sent by the confederated northern tribes in the previous December finally arrived before Congress.[13] In the existing state of affairs Congress could hardly ignore the Indian request for a new treaty, even though the Indians were hoping to win back the land lost in the treaties of 1784-1786. Congress therefore took the opportunity to act on Knox's report of July 10 and on July 21, 1787, resolved that the northern Indians be invited to negotiate a treaty of peace. At the same time it was directed that American troops should be placed in the best possible positions for the defense of the frontiers. On this same day, as Congress was acting on his report of the 10th, Knox presented another report inspired by the Indian message received a few days before. After saying that a confederacy had obviously been formed among most of the tribes northwest of the Ohio, he announced that either war or a treaty was now inevitable. As the United States had no money for a war, Knox suggested that a general treaty with the Indians should be carried out in accordance with the suggestion of the confederated Indians of the Northwest. "A recurrence to the custom of Britain on this point will evince," wrote Knox, "that they thought a treaty and purchase money for land, was the most prudent measure and in no degree dishonorable to the nation." The super confidence of the postwar period was crumbling under the realities of Indian resistance.[14]

The problems of the South were adding to Knox's burden in this solemn July of 1787. On the 18th, in a brief interlude between his two reports on northern Indian affairs, Knox turned his attention to the South—an area about which he was even more pessimistic. After affirming that the Creeks and Georgia were practically at war, he stated that however important it might be to prevent bloodshed "an interference by the United States, seems to be attended with peculiar embarrassments." Knox pointed out that though the Creeks were an independent tribe and not members of the state of Georgia, the state did have legislative jurisdiction over the territory in dispute, and this effectively prevented intervention by the federal government. In fact, Knox asserted, the lack of land cessions prevented all effectual United States intervention in disputes between the independent Indians and the inhabitants of North Carolina and Georgia. Accordingly, Knox urged Congress to press for the liberal cession of western claims by those states to the United States. As it was, Knox admitted that the United States-Cherokee treaty signed at Hopewell in November 1785 had been flagrantly violated by the usurpation of lands assigned to the Cherokee as hunting grounds. To conclude his report Knox pointed out that there was the greatest reason to believe that a general confederacy of the southern Indians was likely, just as there already was a general northern confederacy under Joseph Brant. Unless the United States really possessed the power to manage all affairs with "the independent tribes of Indians" then a general Indian war might be expected.[15]

Congress was deluged with bad news regarding Indian affairs in July and August 1787, and in a desire to avoid war it gradually joined Knox in abandoning the unrealistic methods of the 1783-1786 period. On July 26 another committee reported that mutual depredations were occurring on the frontiers, that settlers as well as Indians were to blame, and that all unauthorized persons should be prevented from travelling northwest of the Ohio. The committee also recommended that particular attention should be paid to state laws protecting Indian rights. There was no positive action on this, but the move to appease the Indians gained momentum.[16]

On August 3 the southern Indians were again the subject of a committee report to Congress. This report, in the writing of Nathan Dane of Massachusetts, stated that encroachments were being made on the lands of the Creeks and the Cherokees by the people of Georgia and North Carolina and that, as there was no regular trade between the United States and the

Indians for goods and arms, the Indians were turning to another quarter (Spain) for these necessities. The committee recommended an inquiry into the causes of hostilities and added "that Justice and policy as well as the true interests of our citizens, evince the propriety of promoting peace and free trade between them and the Indians." The committee then bluntly asserted that "the Indians, in general, within the United States want only to enjoy their lands without interruption, and to have their necessities regularly supplied by our traders, and could these objects be effected, no other measures would, probably be necessary for securing peace and a profitable trade with those Indians. . . . An avaricious disposition in some of our people to acquire large tracts of land and often by unfair means, appears to be the principal source of difficulties with the Indians."

The report next attacked Georgia and North Carolina for their claims of state sovereignty in Indian affairs. "The committee conceive," it was stated, "that it has long been the opinion of the country, supported by Justice and humanity, that the Indians have just claims to all lands occupied by and not fairly purchased from them; and that in managing affairs with them, the principal objects have been those of making war and peace, purchasing certain tracts of their lands, fixing the boundaries between them and our people, and preventing the latter settling on lands left in possession of the former." These powers, argued the committee, were indivisible; they belonged either entirely to the Union or entirely to the state. These powers had belonged to the King before the Revolution, and in the view of the committee they now belonged to the Union. Georgia and North Carolina should either make liberal land cessions to the United States or agree to Congress managing exclusively all affairs with the Cherokees, Creeks, and other independent tribes within the limits of those states. The committee considered, like Henry Knox, that a cession of land claims would be the simplest means of securing these objects. Though this report was not acted upon, it showed quite clearly the developing realization that ruthless aggrandisement would have to be succeeded by a far less direct form of frontier advance.[17]

The argument to alter the course pursued since 1783 reached a peak in another committee report on the northern Indians on August 9, 1787. It was first argued that the Indians were uneasy at the actions of surveyors and settlers beyond the Ohio, that an extensive confederacy had been formed under the influence of Joseph Brant, that the Indians were dissatisfied with the form in which treaties had lately been conducted, and that the confederated tribes wanted to deal collectively with the United States. The committee conceived that there were only two possible courses to silence Indian objections over the manner in which lands northwest of the Ohio had been obtained by the United States: The United States could either wage a vigorous war or hold a general treaty conference and validate the earlier treaties. The committee candidly argued: "The Indians appear to act a natural part for men in their situation . . ., and the Committee are not convinced that a war, under present circumstances, would be consistent with Justice or humanity, but whether so or not, clear it is, that it cannot be consistent with the Interest and policy of the Union." War would be expensive, and its objects could be obtained with one hundredth part the trouble and expense by peaceful means; peace and a regular trade, stated the committee, were clearly the objects to be pursued.

The committee then expressed the view that the measures lately adopted for treating with the Indians were not the best for the objects in view, but that these measures could easily be changed. Practical suggestions followed. General treaties, where all interests could be considered, would be better than treaties with individual tribes. Presents should not be lavished on "all kinds of people" in the tribes but should be reserved for the chiefs and "respectable men." Also "tools of husbandry" could be given to those tribes disposed to live by agriculture. Moreover, "instead of a language of superiority and command; may it not be politic and Just to treat with the Indians more on a footing of equality, convince them of the

Justice and humanity as well as the power of the United States and of their disposition to promote the happiness of the Indians? and instead of attempting to give lands to the Indians to proceed on the principle of fairly purchasing of them and taking the usual deeds?" The committee recommended that general treaty negotiations be held with the northwest Indians as soon after April 1 as possible.[18]

After the soul-searching reports and recommendations of July and August 1787 the United States was ready to turn from a policy of overt dictation and accept the point of view expressed in the August 9 committee report. In many cases treaties were still imposed upon the Indians, but the United States was henceforth at least to go through the motions of formal purchase of Indian rights.

In the Old Northwest the waning years of the Confederation brought a determined effort to persuade the Indians to reconfirm the cessions made in the years 1784-1786. In October 1787 Congress resolved that a general treaty conference should be held with the northwest tribes as soon after April 1, 1788, as possible and, what was more surprising, empowered the Governor of the Northwest Territory, Arthur St. Clair, to spend up to fourteen thousand dollars to secure this object.[19]

The willingness of Congress to expend more money on attaining a peace with the Indians reflected not only the increased danger of Indian hostilities and the gradual change to a principle of purchase, but also the fact that in the summer of 1787 Congress had taken the first major step toward using the lands of the Old Northwest as a source of revenue. Sale of lands under the Ordinance of 1785 began in 1787, and between September 21 and October 9, 1787, 108,431 acres were sold in New York for $176,090, though owing to non-payments Congress eventually received only about two-thirds of this sum. More important were sales made to private land companies. Congress sold some 1,500,000 acres to the Ohio Company of Associates at eight or nine cents per acre; the company paid $500,000 down and the rest in installments.

As a part of the same arrangement with Congress, some 5,000,-000 acres of land northwest of the Ohio were reserved for the Scioto Company. Congress had thus arranged for the sale of some 6,500,000 acres in what is now southern Ohio.[20]

The huge sale to the Ohio Company was the signal for other applications for land in the Old Northwest in the fall of 1787, and some members of Congress began to show, temporarily, a trifle more optimism in regard to United States finances.[21] Yet, to the Indians these sales were disastrous. Indian hopes of an Ohio boundary were rendered impossible of realization as the government contracted for the sale of large areas of land northwest of the Ohio River. Moreover, land in southern Ohio that had not been sold was, for the most part, already set aside as military bounties for the reward of soldiers who had served in the Revolutionary War. The Virginia act of cession to Congress in March 1784 had reserved an area which became known as the "Virginia Military District." This was to be used for the satisfaction of land warrants issued by Virginia for military service during the Revolution. The United States assumed this Virginia land obligation and ordered that no part of the lands northwest of the Ohio between the Little Miami and the Scioto rivers was to be sold until the claims of the servicemen had been satisfied. The United States was in no position to listen to Indian claims for an Ohio River boundary.[22]

Moreover, though Congress had spoken of the need for appeasing the Indians, the government had not lessened its desires for western expansion. The instructions for a treaty in the Northwest, which were sent to Arthur St. Clair on October 26, 1787, left no doubt of American intentions. Though it was asserted that the primary object of the treaty was the establishment of peace and harmony between the United States and the Indians, St. Clair could only depart from previous treaties to obtain a change of boundary beneficial to the United States. Also, though it was asserted that the purchase of the Indian right of soil was not the primary object of the treaty, St. Clair was not to neglect any opportunity that might arise of extinguishing Indian rights as far west as the Mississippi River. If he could do this, it was suggested that a possible boundary might be a westward extension of the southern boundary of Pennsylvania. This line would have placed the southern portions of what are now Ohio, Indiana, and Illinois on the American side of the boundary line. In effect, though Congress had indicated that the overt methods of the 1783-1786 period would have to be modified, the object was still expansion to the Mississippi River.[23]

In the early months of 1788 St. Clair attempted to bring about the treaty desired by Congress, but he encountered frustrating delays. The Indians themselves had waited since December 1786 for Congress to act on their request for a new treaty, and they now had considerable qualms as to the likelihood of achieving their objects through negotiation.[24] At the end of March 1788 Secretary at War Henry Knox argued that no solid peace could be effected with the Indians until the British had given up the northwest posts. He also once again spoke of the financial difficulties that faced the Confederation and stated that he did not think the average number of troops on the frontier could exceed three hundred and fifty during that year.[25] Western lands had not proved a panacea for America's financial woes.

These difficulties and the depressing news from the Northwest made Knox even more certain that the Confederation Government had been mistaken in its policy in the immediate postwar years. On May 2 he was particularly blunt in reporting the northwestern situation to Congress. The Indians of the Northwest, reported Knox, were disgusted at "the principle of conquest" which had been used to acquire their lands in the 1784-1786 treaties. The only method to which they would peaceably agree, he argued, would be formal sale of the Indian "right of the soil," the practice they had become accustomed to with the British and most of the northern colonies in the colonial period. Accordingly, Knox asserted that it would be foolish in the coming treaty to bind the commissioner to asserting "the principle of conquest." The maintenance of this principle would call for continual warfare. "Your Secretary humbly apprehends," wrote Knox, "that the United States may conform to the modes and customs of the indians in the disposal of their lands, without the least injury to the national dignity." Knox's conclusion was that the instructions for a new northwestern treaty should be modified to allow purchasing Indian claims to lands already obtained by the United States in the 1784-1786 treaties. This was necessary, argued Knox, because "an extensive indian war in the present political crisis, and with an exhausted treasury, would be an event pregnant with unlimited evil." [26]

On July 2, 1788, additional resolutions were passed by Congress regarding the negotiations to be held with the western Indians. Now twenty thousand dollars was added to the original appropriation of fourteen thousand for the expenses of St. Clair's negotiations with the tribes of the Old Northwest. Congress stipulated that this twenty thousand plus six thousand of the money already appropriated by Congress was to be used solely to purchase Indian claims to the lands they had already ceded to the United States, "by obtaining regular conveyances for the same, and for extending a purchase beyond the limits hitherto fixed by treaty." [27] Yet, the actual instructions which were sent to St. Clair as a result of these resolutions suggested a boundary even more advantageous to the United States. Whereas in the previous October an extension westward of the southern boundary of Pennsylvania had been suggested as a possible dividing line, now it was suggested that the forty-first degree of north latitude might be used. The former line would have left the greater part of the present state of Ohio to the Indians; the latter would have given by far the greater part of that state to the United States. The desire for land did not diminish.[28]

Arthur St. Clair clearly realized that the proposed treaty would fail if he was forced to ask for the forty-first parallel as a boundary, and as soon as he received his instructions containing this suggestion he objected in a letter to the Secretary at War. He said that even the first east-west line—a line westward from the southern boundary of Pennsylvania—would not be secured without the greatest difficulty and that the line of the forty-first parallel was completely impractical. On August 12, 1788, Congress acknowledged St. Clair's difficulties when it resolved that owing to the very hostile appearance of the Indians it was necessary for the frontiers to be put into a state of defense and for the instructions to the commissioners to be modified so that in further purchases of Indian rights to land the commissioners should have the power to adjust the boundaries as they thought best.[29]

Since the Indians had met in general council in December 1786, they had been preparing, with the encouragement of the British, to meet the demands of the Americans. At first the Indians had been anxious for a prompt meeting with the United States, but after her delay the Indians themselves held back as they attempted to formulate a policy with which to confront the Americans.[30] In the fall of 1788 the Indians again met in general council, but they found great difficulty in uniting on specific demands. The Miami, Shawnee, and Kickapoo wished to yield nothing and continue hostilities.[31] Finally, however, the Iroquois sent a message to St. Clair on behalf of the confederated tribes. They proposed that the earlier treaties should be disregarded and that American settlement should be allowed only as far as the Muskingum River in what is now eastern Ohio.[32] St. Clair immediately rejected this proposal. Moreover, he reiterated a statement that Congress had been avoiding in the late 1780's that Great Britain had disposed of the Indian country at the peace treaty in 1783. St. Clair's rejection of this preliminary Indian proposal was enough to dissuade Joseph Brant, his Mohawks, and the Wabash tribes from coming in to negotiate with the Americans. The Six Nations replied to St. Clair and denied that their land had been given up by the British in 1783. They also denied that they now expected assistance from the British: "We do not put more confidence in them than we do in any other civilized Nations who we know have always their own interest in view." [33]

At long last, in the middle of December 1788, a group of some two hundred Iroquois (without the Mohawks), Wyandots, Delawares, Ottawas, Chippewas, and Potawatomis came into Fort Harmar. After two weeks of preliminary negotiations, in which the Indians demonstrated their lack of unity, the British-American peace treaty of 1783 was read and explained to the Indians on December 28. On the following day an Indian proposal for an Ohio River boundary was put before St. Clair. In a brief reply St. Clair stated that he could not deviate from the treaties concluded at Fort Stanwix, Fort McIntosh, and at the mouth of the Great Miami. The Indians then retreated a little and suggested a boundary at the Muskingum. On January 6 St. Clair delivered a full reply to the Indian proposals. In the face of Indian resistance his language took on the coloring of the 1783-1786 period rather than that of Congress since 1787. He told the Indians that their land had been ceded to the United States by Great Britain in 1783 and that the division of land at Fort Stanwix, Fort McIntosh, and the mouth of the Great Miami had been an act of clemency on the part of the United States. He did, however, offer to pay the Indians for agreeing to the earlier treaties and stated that if they would renew and confirm the Fort McIntosh boundary an article would be inserted in the treaty confirming the Indian right to hunt on the land east of the boundary. Though St. Clair was proposing purchase, he was still in effect dictating the treaty that would be signed. In its recommendations for appeasing the Indians, Congress had not allowed for what would have to be done if the Indians took no more happily to the idea of selling their lands than they had to the idea of yielding them for nothing. In the long run, of course, forced purchase was no more palatable than forced cession.[34]

On January 9, 1789, two treaties were signed at Fort Harmar. The first treaty was with the Wyandots, Delawares, Ottawas, Potawatomis, and Sac tribes and confirmed the boundary established at the Treaty of Fort McIntosh in 1785, "to the end that the same may remain as a division line between the lands of the United States of America, and the lands of said nations, forever." For this confirmation the United States agreed to give goods to the value of six thousand dollars. Though by Article II the boundary line had been confirmed "forever," Article III gave the right of pre-emption of the Indian lands to the United States. The assumptions of the 1780's and the instructions to St. Clair prior to this treaty made it obvious that Article III rather than Article II had the ultimate significance.[35]

The second treaty signed at Fort Harmar was that with the Six Nations. By this treaty the Six Nations confirmed the Fort Stanwix Treaty of October 1784. For this confirmation the United States agreed to give goods to the value of three thousand dollars. The lands of the Six Nations were confirmed to them, but there was no need for a clause granting pre-emption to the United States, for the lands of the Six Nations lay within the state of New York, and the national frontier had passed them by.[36]

Though the treaty at Fort Harmar had at least introduced the principle of purchase by having the United States pay (a nominal sum) for lands already obtained from the Indians in 1784 and 1785, it had not really differed greatly from those earlier treaties. The truly dissatisfied Indians had not attended the negotiations at all, and those who had attended had been pressured into yielding more than they had wished. Though Congress from 1787 had talked of dealing with the Indians more equally and formally purchasing lands, St. Clair had ruthlessly overridden Indian objections when they had attempted to change the course of the treaty. As a result, St. Clair obtained a confirmation of the treaties of 1784 and 1785 in spite of widespread Indian opposition to those treaties in the period from 1785 to 1789. He had failed, of course, in any attempt to obtain even more land in the Northwest but this still remained the ultimate aim. In a report to President Washington in May 1789 he excused this lack of success with the arguments that it would have been difficult to explain to the Indians what was meant by a boundary along the forty-first parallel and that he had discovered that "any Attempt to extend the limits at that time would be very ill received, if not defeat entirely the settling a Peace with them; it was therefore not proposed, and the Boundaries remained as settled at the former Treaties except the rectifying an Error about the Portage at the Miami Village." [37]

The Treaties of Fort Harmar were the culmination of confederation Indian policy in the Old Northwest. St. Clair hoped he had established peace, confirmed American possession of lands beyond the Ohio River, and provided for settlement. He was wrong. The Indians were as affronted by the Treaties of Fort Harmar as by the other treaties of the 1780's. The treaties hardly interrupted the flow of Indian hostilities, and the new federal government was confronted with a breakdown of American Indian policy northwest of the Ohio River.

Indian affairs in the South were also in a state of chaos from 1787 to 1789. The attempts of Congress to conciliate the Indian tribes and establish definite boundaries had seemed futile even as they were being made in 1785 and 1786, and the states and citizens of Georgia and North Carolina flouted Congressional policies in these last years of the Confederation. The federal government failed in its efforts to moderate the Indian policies of the southern states.

These years brought tension and sporadic hostilities. By the fall of 1787 a war between Georgia and the Creeks seemed certain, and Congress decided that another treaty should be signed to preserve peace with the southern tribes. It was resolved that North Carolina, South Carolina, and Georgia should each appoint commissioners to act with the superintendent for the southern Indians in negotiating a treaty. The instructions of the commissioners stated that North Carolina and the Cherokees, and Georgia and the Creeks were either already fighting or on the eve of war and that the great sources of contention were boundaries. They were to ascertain the boundaries claimed by the respective states because, though Congress thought it might constitutionally fix the boundaries, it did not want the states to feel their legislative rights were being violated. The principal object of the treaty was to be the restoration of peace; no cession of land was to be demanded of the Indian tribes. Every effort was to be made to discover the real leaders of the tribes and attach them to the United States by kind treatment, assurances of protection, and "presents of a permanent Nature." These instructions were hardly designed to illuminate the task of the commissioners. Though it was asserted that no further cessions of land were to be demanded, it was also declared that the claims of the states were to be respected. No provision was made for reconciling differences when the Indians did not acknowledge treaties and boundaries negotiated by the states earlier in the decade or for occasions when state claims differed from earlier federal delineations of the boundaries.[38]

All this hardly proved a problem as the Confederation now showed its usual dilatoriness and, indeed, expired before another federal treaty was made with the southern tribes. Throughout 1788 Secretary at War Henry Knox bewailed the ineffectiveness of federal Indian policy and the necessity for some new arrangement. For the most part he was markedly pessimistic. On May 26, he reported that the United States-Cherokee Treaty of Hopewell, signed in November 1785, had repeatedly been violated by the frontier inhabitants, and he observed that in spite of the Congressional resolutions of October 26, 1787, which had called for a treaty with the southern tribes, North Carolina had not yet appointed a commissioner. Knox further developed his accusations against the frontier inhabitants in a report of July 18, 1788. He stated that the white inhabitants on the frontiers of North Carolina, in the vicinity of Chota on the Tennessee River, had frequently committed "the most unprovoked and direct outrages against the Cherokee Indians." Knox minced no words on this matter: "the unjustifiable conduct of the said inhabitants has most probably been dictated by the avaricious desire of obtaining the fertile lands possessed by the said indians of which and particularly of their ancient town of Chota they are exceedingly tenacious." Knox specifically attacked the conduct of the state of Franklin. He thought it essential that Congress should enforce the Hopewell Treaty and that settlers should be removed from the Indian lands by force if necessary. It was essential, urged Knox, that the Indian tribes rely with confidence on their treaties with the United States. Otherwise the southern frontiers would be constantly embroiled in war, and "all the other tribes will have good grounds not only according to their own opinions but according to the impartial judgments of the civilized part of the human race for waging perpetual war against the citizens of the United States." [39]

The tale of woe continued. On July 28 Knox reported that if the Creeks would not enter a reasonable treaty the United States would have to try to win in one effective campaign or risk a long, expensive, and inglorious war. He pointed out that the Creeks were much stronger than the Wabash Indians and that the United States would need a force of two thousand eight hundred men for nine months. The estimated cost for all this was $450,000, an exceedingly large sum for the Confederation in the summer of 1788. Two days after this depressing report on the Creeks, a committee of Congress endorsed Knox's view on the Cherokee situation. They reiterated his statements about the outrages committed by the inhabitants on the frontiers of North Carolina and pointed out that this was in open violation of the Treaty of Hopewell. The committee considered that the United States should interpose to enforce the treaty and suggested that the Secretary at War have troops ready to march from the Ohio River to disperse American intruders. These suggestions were not acted upon until September 1 when Congress agreed to a proclamation forbidding violations of the Treaty of Hopewell and ordering intruders to leave Indian lands. It was asserted, however, that nothing in the proclamation should affect the territorial claims of North Carolina. Congress also resolved that the Secretary at War should have troops ready to march from the Ohio and the copies of this action should be sent to the executives of Virginia and North Carolina. The violations in the vicinity of Chota were also referred to the executive of North Carolina for investigation and punishment of the guilty.[40]

Congressional action in the fall of 1788 was merely the last twitch of an already dead body. The Confederation had failed in its efforts to impose a federal Indian policy upon the South. Georgia, North Carolina, and the temporary state of Franklin had pursued their own policies and had thwarted Congressional efforts to bring some order into southern Indian affairs. The Confederation had failed to achieve a treaty with the Creeks, and its Hopewell Treaty with the Cherokees had been constantly violated by settlers on the frontiers of North Carolina. Congress had wanted to pacify the South to clear the path for expansion in the North, but found the powers of the Confederation too limited to attain this desired object. It remained for the new national government to bring some order into the course of the western advance and into plans for overcoming the aborigines who opposed it.

The Aims of the
New Government

IV

THE ESTABLISHMENT of a new federal government in the
spring of 1789 brought renewed and more vigorous discussion of American Indian policy. The Secretary of War, Henry
Knox, now expanded the ideas he had first suggested in the
last years of the Confederation and tried to bring a new respectability into the conduct of American-Indian relations. In
this endeavor he was aided by President Washington. Both
Knox and Washington placed far greater emphasis on the
morality of American policy than had been common for most
of the Confederation period.

On May 25, 1789, Washington submitted to the Senate a
report from the Secretary of War on the Treaties of Fort
Harmar. For the information of the new Congress the report
listed the treaties made with the Indians of the Old Northwest
since 1783 and informed the new Senate that "the Indians are
greatly tenacious of their lands, and generally do not relin-

quish their right, excepting on the principle of a specific consideration expressly given for the purchase of the same." Knox pointed out that the American colonies and the British had established the habit of purchasing Indian claims and that this habit could not be violated except with difficulty and at great expense. He also argued that the Treaties of Fort Stanwix and Fort McIntosh had been opposed because they had not acknowledged the principle of purchase and that as a result Congress had appropriated money for new negotiations.[1] Thus the new Congress was told at its inception that the Indians expected a formal purchase of land. The changes in policy which had gradually been effected since 1787 were now to receive more formal expression.

In June and July of 1789 Henry Knox made two significant statements on American-Indian policy. As Secretary of War since 1785, Knox had long been aware of the difficulties of carrying out an effective Indian policy. He came into office as the confident claims of post-1783 were being challenged by the Indians, and he had observed the fruits of a policy of naked aggrandisement. He had also seen American-Indian policy in the South rendered impotent by the obdurant attitude of the states and by the settlers' disregard for any Indian rights. As a soldier, he could see no real honor in an Indian war. He could see only difficulty, expense, and tedious guerrilla warfare. Knox wanted a proud, powerful nation and an orderly westward advance, and he thought that this could be achieved by federal control and a more humane Indian policy.

In a report on June 15 Knox commented first on the hostility of the Wabash tribes. To put an end to this open hostility the United States could either raise an army and extirpate the hostiles, or hold treaties in which Indian rights and limits would be clearly defined. Even if the force were available, Knox asserted, it would be a matter of debate whether the United States could, consistent with principles of justice and "the laws of nature," undertake the expulsion or destruction of the tribes on the Wabash: "It is presumable," wrote Knox, "that a nation solicitous of establishing its character on the broad basis of justice, would not only hesitate at, but reject every proposition to benefit itself, by the injury of any neighboring community, however contemptible and weak it might be, either with respect to its manners or power." After stating that even expulsion would ultimately bring about the destruction of the Indians, as they would thereby encroach on the hunting grounds of other tribes and be destroyed by war, Knox presented a concept of Indian rights that had been ignored for most of the Confederation period: "The Indians being the prior occupants, possess the right of the soil. It cannot be taken from them unless by their free consent, or by the right of conquest in case of a just war. To dispossess them on any other principle, would be a gross violation of the fundamental laws of nature, and of that distributive justice which is the glory of a nation." The only disturbing note in this firm statement of principle was the provision for "the right of conquest in case of a just war." All wars are just in the eyes of the nation that fights them, and as the Indians would undoubtedly resist the cession of large areas of land, this provision could come in for considerable use.

After stressing principle, Knox next indicated the practical aspects of his policy. Even if it were decided to expel the Indians by force, Knox asserted, the United States could not afford it. Both justice and necessity made negotiations desirable. Only if negotiations failed should an attempt be made to punish the Indians. "The time has arrived," stated Knox, "when it is highly expedient that a liberal system of justice should be adopted for the various Indian tribes within the limits of the United States." He surveyed the Congressional attitude in the 1780's and concluded that after 1783 Congress was of the opinion that the Peace Treaty of 1783 absolutely invested the United States with the full title of all Indian lands within the limits of the United States. The Indians, on the other hand, considered that they were the proprietors of the soil, and the Confederation Congress had eventually conformed to this belief by appropriating money in 1788 solely for the purpose of extinguishing Indian claims to lands already ceded to the United States. "The principle of the Indian right to the lands they possess being thus conceded," stated Knox, "the dignity and interest of the nation will be advanced by making it the basis of the future administration of justice towards the Indian tribes." To attach the Indians north and south of the Ohio to the United States for the next fifty years might cost fifteen thousand dollars a year, thought Knox. To coerce them would cost far more and would also stain the character of the nation "beyond all pecuniary calculation."

Moreover, and here Knox reasserted the idea that had been the basis of the advice of Philip Schuyler and Washington in 1783, a policy of peace, honor, and conciliation would not mean the end of expansion. "As the settlements of the whites shall approach near to the Indian boundaries established by treaties," wrote Knox, "the game will be diminished, and the lands being valuable to the Indians only as hunting grounds, they will be willing to sell further tracts for small considerations. By the expiration, therefore, of the above period [fifty years], it is most probable that the Indians will, by the invariable operation of the causes which have hitherto existed in their intercourse with the whites, be reduced to a very small number." As had Schuyler and Washington before him, Knox failed to realize that the Indians would fight when existing boundaries were threatened by the advance of American settlement. The policy was to be very similar to that suggested in 1783, with the exception that there was now to be no large initial cession as a payment for Indian activities during the Revolution. Instead, the United States would pay for a solemn conveyance of each tract of land. It was always assumed, however, that the Indians would be willing to sell. The policy did not allow for a situation in which the Indians desired to resist any American advance, whether by war or purchase.[2]

Less than a month later, in July 1789, in a report which was concerned mainly with the southern Indians, Knox used substantially the same arguments as in his June 15 report. He attacked the "disgraceful violation" of the Hopewell Treaty with the Cherokees and once again laid down his philosophy of peaceful expansion. He argued that though the emigration of Americans into Indian country could not be effectually prevented, it could be restrained by a postponement of new purchases of Indian lands. Yet, he reiterated his belief that this would simplify expansion as the population increased and approached Indian boundaries. But he differed from his predecessors in lamenting rather than praising the results of this development: "It is, however, painful to consider, that all the Indian tribes, once existing in those States now the best cultivated and most populous, have become extinct. If the same causes continue, the same effects will happen; and, in a short period, the idea of an Indian on this side the Mississippi will only be found in the page of the historian."

Knox argued strongly for the necessity of federal control over treaty making and stated that "the independent nations and tribes of Indians ought to be considered as foreign nations, not as the subjects of any particular State." This idea of regarding the Indian tribes as foreign nations rather than a domestic problem, a concept which was later to be looked upon as a weakness in American Indian policy, arose to a great extent from the peculiarities of the federal system. It was essential, particularly in the South, to win away control of Indian affairs from the southern states, and one of the ways to accomplish this was to regard the Indians as sovereign nations and therefore objects of American national foreign policy. Knox, in this report of 1789, at the very birth of the American government, was willing to concede that the individual states would have to retain the pre-emption of all lands within their limits, but he defended the supremacy of the federal government in treaties and boundaries which would inevitably decide the question of peace or war. In this way the federal government could at least exercise some control over expansion and relations with the Indians rather than allowing unrestrained state expansion which would spark continual Indian hostilities.

Finally in his report of July 1789 Knox bespoke his faith in the natural man and his capabilities for improvement. In doing so he foreshadowed the great emphasis which was to be placed on bringing civilization to the Indians in this first phase of the new American national government from 1789 to 1812. If expansion, as Knox had indicated, was inevitable, then the only way to prevent the elimination of the Indian was his absorption within American civilization. This seemed an obvious solution. The Indian would give up his lands to the advancing American farmer, but in return he would receive the inestimable gift of civilization. Some such idea had been hinted at in the Confederation period, but now under Washington this notion was to develop into an essential part of the government's Indian policy. Indeed, it was to become its great justification, for if the advancing frontiersman was not merely a ruthless appropriator of land, but was also a carrier of civilization and a better life, then what Knox and others feared would be recorded as a sordid episode would become a noble enterprise: "How different," wrote Knox, "would be the sensation of a philosophic mind to reflect, that, instead of exterminating a part of the human race by our modes of population, we had persevered, through all difficulties, and at last had imparted our knowledge of cultivation and the arts to the aboriginals of the country, by which the source of future life and happiness had been preserved and extended."

Knox then quarrelled with those who asserted that it was impracticable to civilize the Indians. "To deny," he said, "that under a course of favorable circumstances, it could not be accomplished, is to suppose the human character under the influence of such stubborn habits as to be incapable of melioration or change—a supposition entirely contradicted by the progress of society, from the barbarous ages to its present degree of perfection." [3] The boundless optimism in the "present degree of perfection" encouraged the belief that the Indians would inevitably realize that they were being given a great opportunity by the advance of the American frontier. This idea of the colonizer bringing the chance for perfection of society to the aborigines formed a continuous thread in nineteenth-century expansion, and it provided the supreme justification for a policy which in its crudest form merely seemed to be eliminating the aboriginal populations to make room for the Europeans. Washington echoed the sentiments of Knox in a message to the Senate on August 7, 1789, when he asserted that "while the measures of Government ought to be calculated to protect its citizens from all injury and violence, a due regard should be extended to those Indian tribes whose happiness in the course of events so materially depends on the national justice and humanity of the United States." [4]

With the coming of a new government the United States leaders felt a great determination to improve the American image in the eyes of the world. This determination, however, was not only a question of morality; it was also a question of policy. The directness of the 1780's had brought only Indian war. If the United States were to advance across the continent with a minimum of difficulty, it was considered essential that the Indians accept rather than reject American intentions. Advance could still take place, but it would proceed in the face of sporadic rather than continual Indian wars, and the wars would be interspersed with the granting of "permanent" boundaries to the Indians, which at least temporarily would be protected by the United States against the encroachments of her own citizens. Yet, as in the 1780's, the policy in action proved more unpredictable than the policy in theory. Both in the North and South the Indians were to show ability in discerning the long-range rather than the temporary objectives of the American government.

In his two administrations from 1789 to 1797 Washington, guided by Knox until 1795, urged the application of this new and more humane policy in American-Indian relations. War hindered expansion and brought discredit on the nation. If the United States could formally purchase land from the Indians and establish boundaries, if these boundaries could then be protected against white encroachment by the edict and force of the American government, if unruly offenders against the Indians could be punished by American law, then the

United States could hope to establish an orderly frontier advance. If as a corollary to these controls an extensive trade could be established and the Indians introduced to the methods and ideas of western civilization, then the United States would become a benefactor and not an oppressor. The United States would advance westward, but it would advance peacefully and bring civilization. All this, of course, depended on the Indians accepting the American idea that they would be better off as a result of American expansion and, furthermore, upon expansion proceeding cautiously enough that the Indians would not be alienated before they had even begun to be acculturated. Neither of these *sine qua non* proved possible. The Indians rejected the idea of giving up their way of life, and the American frontier pressed forward with relentless speed. Yet, in these first two administrations under the Constitution, the government took firm steps to enforce obedience of treaties and boundary lines, to open a regular trade, and to introduce civilization among the Indians through agriculture, spinning, and weaving. These efforts took place in spite of widespread Indian hostilities.

In his Third Annual Message of October 25, 1791, though Washington spoke of the need for military action against the hostile tribes (the United States was to suffer a crushing defeat within two weeks), he went on to argue, "It is sincerely to be desired that all need of coercion in future may cease and that an intimate intercourse may succeed, calculated to advance the happiness of the Indians and to attach them firmly to the United States." In order to achieve this end Washington thought that the Indians should receive impartial justice, their method of alienating land should be regulated and defined, commerce with them should be encouraged, experiments should be made to bring the "blessings of civilization," the executive should be empowered to dispense gifts, and violators of Indian rights should be punished. In short, "A system corresponding with the mild principles of religion and philanthropy toward an unenlightened race of men, whose happiness materially depends on the conduct of the United States, would be as honorable to the national character as conformable to the dictates of sound policy." [5]

The military disaster suffered at the hands of the Indians in the Northwest in November 1791 did not change these sentiments. In 1792 both Washington and Knox reiterated their belief in a humane Indian policy. In his Fourth Annual Message in November 1792 Washington recommended adequate laws to prevent outrages against the Indians, adequate money to hire Indian agents, and a suitable plan "for promoting civilization among the friendly tribes" and carrying on trade with them without extortion. Washington thought the Indians should be wooed rather than coerced, and he had suggested to the Senate some nine months earlier that in managing the Indians "it appears proper to teach them to expect annual presents, conditioned on the evidence of their attachment to the interests of the United States." [6]

Henry Knox, more than Washington, appeared perturbed by the thought of how American policy would appear to present and future generations. In a speech he sent to the northwestern Indians in April 1792 he said that the Indian belief that the United States wanted to deprive them of their lands and drive them out of the country was not true; "on the contrary, . . . we should be greatly gratified with the opportunity of imparting to you all the blessings of civilized life, of teaching you to cultivate the earth, and raise corn; to raise oxen, sheep, and other domestic animals; to build comfortable houses, and to educate your children, so as ever to dwell upon the land." In the following month Knox instructed Envoy Rufus Putnam that "the United States are highly desirous of imparting to all the Indian tribes, the blessings of civilization, as the only means of perpetuating them on the earth." Knox had a clear realization of how American expansion would be viewed. "If our modes of population and War destroy the tribes," he wrote to Anthony Wayne in January 1793, "the disinterested part of mankind and posterity will be apt to class the effects of our Conduct and that of the Spaniards in Mexico and Peru together." [7]

The suggestions of Washington and Knox had practical results in the early years of the new government. Through a series of trade and intercourse acts direct efforts were made to force American citizens to observe the boundaries established by treaties with the Indians. It was hoped to prevent continued warfare by allowing white-Indian contact only under strict regulation. Moreover, if the Indians could be convinced of the good intentions of the American government in regard to the protection of established boundaries, then peace would be preserved, and American settlement could proceed rapidly on the land which had already been ceded. Such expansion on the American side of the boundary would then, as Knox and Washington had already agreed, make further cessions comparatively simple. Thus, peace would be established, the worst infringements on Indian rights avoided, the honor of the nation preserved, and the future purchase of Indian lands facilitated.

On July 22, 1790, the first of the trade and intercourse acts was enacted. This measure, which followed the precedents established by the Ordinance of 1786, licensed trade, forbade private purchases of land, and provided for the punishment of whites who committed various crimes in Indian country. On March 1, 1793, the 1790 act was strengthened; specific punishment was provided for anyone settling on Indian land, and the President was empowered to give useful articles to the Indians and appoint temporary agents to promote civilization. To effect these objectives he was authorized to spend twenty thousand dollars a year.

The powers of the President in this regard were again strengthened on May 19, 1796. This act specifically delineated the boundaries of the Indian country and gave the President power to use force against illegal settlers on Indian lands. It was particularly directed against southern encroachments on the land of the Cherokees and Creeks. The provisions of the 1793 act for bringing civilization to the Indians were also continued, but the appropriation was cut to fifteen thousand dollars a year; with this sum, and any special appropriation provided for in the treaties, it was hoped to bring the Indians within the mainstream of American life. The Act of 1796 (which was substantially re-enacted in 1799) was the basis of American-Indian relations in this regard until Jefferson's measure of March 1802. These acts were designed to protect the American Indian, but it can also be argued that they were designed to facilitate rather than restrict American expansion.[8]

Congress also eventually acted upon Washington's repeated requests for a systematic method of trade with the Indian tribes and in April 1796 established the factory system. This measure provided for the establishment of government trading factories which would deal fairly with the Indians. The object was not to make a profit, but merely to provide for Indian wants without extortion or fraud. It was hoped that through this plan the Indians would be wooed away from foreign traders, become attached to the interests of the United States, and protected from the sometimes fraudulent private traders. The system lasted until 1822, but it never had the force that had been hoped for. Private traders continued to ply their wares among the Indian tribes, often ignoring federal efforts to prevent liquor reaching the Indians, and the government trading factories achieved only limited success.[9]

By 1796, however, Washington could well claim that he had achieved a series of regulations designed to curb the more blatant excesses of American-Indian relations. Washington and Knox had publicly stated their belief in a fair and proper purchase of the Indian right of soil, had advocated the protection of Indian boundaries, and had urged the administration of equal justice for white and Indian alike. They had also shown a definite awareness of how outsiders and future generations were likely to view American Indian policy and a realization of how important the issue was for the national honor. In his Annual Message of December 1795 Washington spoke of the possibility of civilizing the Indians, arguing, "The accomplishment of this work, if practicable, will reflect undecaying luster on our national character and administer the most grateful consolations that virtuous minds can know." [10] Knox, who resigned at the end of 1794, well summarized the changes in American policy in his final report and political testament on December 29 of that year. He argued that since 1789 the government had striven not only to form treaties of peace with the Indians on principles of justice, but also "to impart to them all the blessings of civilized life of which their condition is susceptible." A perseverance in such principles, he thought, would "reflect permanent honor upon the national character," but he admitted that the carrying into practice of the good intentions was frequently complicated by "perplexing considerations." The major problem here, Knox argued, was the desire of frontiersmen to take Indian lands; this produced hostilities in which the killing of whites was looked upon with more severity than the killing of Indians.

Knox spoke of the evils of Indian war and argued strongly in favor of peace: "The United States can get nothing by an Indian war; but they risk men, money, and reputation. As we are more powerful, and more enlightened than they are, there is a responsibility of national character, that we should treat them with kindness, and even liberality. It is a melancholy reflection, that our modes of population have been more destructive to the Indian natives than the conduct of the conquerors of Mexico and Peru. The evidence of this is the utter extirpation of nearly all the Indians in most populous parts of the Union. A future historian may mark the causes of this destruction of the human race in sable colors." To prevent Indian wars Knox recommended that a line of frontier military posts be established on the Indian side of the boundary (if Indian consent could be obtained), that Indians who committed crimes be delivered up to the nearest military post for trial by court martial, and that any persons who were in the Indian country with the object of inflicting harm on the Indians be liable to punishment by the rules and articles of war for American troops. If this military policing of the frontiers were combined with stimulation of trade and the appointment of agents to reside in the principal Indian towns, Knox argued that "it would seem that the Government would then have made the fairest experiments of a system of justice and humanity, which, it is presumed, could not possibly fail of being blessed with its proper effects—an honorable tranquillity of the frontiers." [11]

Secretary of War Knox and President Washington thus constantly emphasized the new orientation of American policy and the manner in which the new government had based its policies on reasonableness and justice. But what of the practice? How were these good intentions of the early years of the new government carried into effect? Undoubtedly new laws were passed to protect the Indian boundary lines and promote trade with the Indians, but did these bring a new regime in American policy? Were the Indians convinced of the good intentions of the American government? Had the sporadic warfare and bitterness of the 1780's become peaceful acculturation and quiet expansion in the 1790's? The record is a sad one.

The South, 1789—1799

V

THE EXECUTIVE of the new government wasted no time in bringing the problem of the Indians to the attention of the legislature. On August 7, 1789, Washington laid before Congress a considerable body of material relating to both northern and southern Indians. This information had been compiled by Henry Knox and included a number of his reports. His first report on the southern Indians, dated July 6, was concerned with the Creeks and Georgia. He pointed out that hostilities still raged on the Georgia frontier, that the cause of the war was a complete rejection by the Creeks of the three treaties made between them and Georgia from 1783 to 1786, and that the United States, by a Congressional resolve of July 15, 1788, had notified the Creeks that if they would not enter into a treaty on reasonable terms, then military action would be taken to protect the frontier. Knox wanted to know whether or not the United States should now raise an army to fight the Creeks.[1]

A second report on the southern Indians, dated July 7, 1789, dealt with the Cherokees. Knox stated that the United States had entered into a treaty with this tribe at Hopewell in November 1785, that North Carolina had protested that this treaty infringed upon her rights, and that "it has been proved that the said treaty has been entirely disregarded by the white people inhabiting the frontiers, styling themselves the State of Franklin." Knox spoke of "the deplorable situation of the Cherokees, and the indispensable obligation of the United States to vindicate their faith, justice, and national dignity." [2]

A third report on the southern Indians, also dated July 7, dealt with the Chickasaws and Choctaws. The United States, stated Knox, had made treaties with these nations at Hopewell in January 1786, but their distance from the frontier settlements was so great that no complaints had been made of white encroachments. The Chickasaws had, however, indicated their sympathy with the Cherokees.[3] The immediate crisis was the state of relations with the Creeks and Cherokees. After these individual reports concerned with particular southern tribes Knox returned to the more general problems in a longer document, which was also dated July 7, 1789.

Knox first asserted that there was great danger of a general union of the southern tribes, under the leadership of the Creek Alexander McGillivray, and with Spanish support, and that there must be war or negotiation with the Creeks. The first, he believed, would necessitate raising an army of five thousand men and would cost $1,500,000. If, on the other hand, commissioners were appointed, Knox argued that they should be empowered to decide all disputed boundaries between the Creeks and Georgia regardless of previous treaties between the two parties. These commissioners should also be empowered to examine the Cherokee problem, renew the November 1785 Hopewell Treaty and report the measures that would be necessary to protect the Cherokees in their former boundaries. However, even in the event of treaties being signed, Knox considered it essential that five hundred troops be provided to protect the boundaries. In this way paper

promises would be given some force, and the disgraceful violations of the Hopewell Treaty with the Cherokees would not be
repeated. Knox concluded this report with a long argument
for better treatment of the Indians and the necessity of a
guarantee of their rights.[4]

Knox obviously favored another attempt at negotiating
with the southern Indians, and, faced with the estimate of the
cost of war, Congress promptly agreed with him. Washington
quickly nominated three commissioners and on August 22 appeared before the Senate to discuss their instructions. In an
introduction to his questions the President alluded to the necessity of peace with the southern Indians and then asked for
advice from the Senate.[5] From the suggestions of Knox and
Washington, and with Senatorial advice, a set of instructions
was drawn up and sent to the commissioners on August 29.
The instructions were long and detailed.

The first great object of the mission was to be the negotiation and establishment of peace between Georgia and the
Creeks; it was particularly specified that the whole Creek nation be fully represented. The commissioners were to investigate the three Georgia-Creek treaties (Augusta, Galphinton,
and Shoulderbone) and decide whether or not they had been
fairly negotiated. If they had been, the Creeks were to be
urged to confirm them and threatened with punishment if
they refused. If, on the other hand, it was found that the
cessions at those treaties had been obtained unfairly, then the
commissioners were not to insist on their renewal. However,
and here the whole principle of conciliation collapsed, it was
observed that Georgia had proceeded on the assumption that
the cessions at Augusta had been fairly obtained and had
surveyed and divided the land between the Ogeechee and
Oconee rivers. Georgians had settled and planted on these
lands in great numbers. Thus, should the commissioners' in-
vestigation be unfavorable to Georgia, "it would be highly
embarrassing to that State to relinquish the said lands to the
Creeks." This being the case, the commissioners were urged to
persuade the Creeks to yield the land between the Ogeechee

and the Oconee; if necessary, money could be given for this purpose, and it could be pointed out that the disputed lands had already been entirely despoiled of their game by the settlements and were no longer valuable to the Creeks as hunting grounds.

In order to secure peace, and the Ogeechee-Oconee land, the commissioners could also, if necessary, make further stipulations to the Creeks. They could guarantee them a port on the Altamaha River for trade, promise gifts to influential chiefs, and guarantee the remaining Creek lands; these would be protected, if necessary, by a line of military posts. Much attention was paid to the importance of McGillivray, and it was stated that in order to win him away from the Spanish he might be offered an American military rank higher than the one he supposedly held from Spain. If in spite of all this the Creeks still would not yield the Ogeechee-Oconee lands, then a treaty could be signed making the Oconee a temporary boundary. Included in any such treaty should be a stipulation for a number of missionaries to reside among the Creeks to teach religion and morality, and inculcate a friendship for the United States. If the Creeks then refused any treaty, the commissioners should regard them as hostile and report measures for the defense of the frontiers.

The instructions dealt almost exclusively with the Creeks, for it was pointed out in the instructions that though the case of the Cherokees seemed to require the immediate intervention of the United States, most of them resided within the territory claimed by North Carolina, who had not yet joined the Union. Should North Carolina ratify the Constitution, the United States would have to make every effort to carry into effect the Hopewell Treaty of November 1785; in the meantime the commissioners should send the Cherokees a message pointing out the American difficulties. The commissioners were also to send messages to the Choctaws and Chickasaws and were to report a plan to carry on trade with those nations in conformity with the Treaties of Hopewell.

The whole tenor of the instructions was such as to suggest

that it might well be discovered that the three Georgia-Creek treaties should be regarded as invalid, but that in effect Georgia had presented the United States Government with a *fait accompli* in regard to the land between the Ogeechee and the Oconee. As a result, though all the previous discussion had stressed the necessity for conciliation and moderation, the commissioners were placed in the position of pressing for the continuation of a cession of land that had never been made by the majority of the Creek nation. It was also ominous that the guarantee of even the remaining Creek lands was only to be given "if you should find the measure necessary." [6]

American hopes for a quick settlement vanished in the fall of 1789. After a fruitless journey to Georgia the commissioners were obliged to report to Knox on November 20 that the Creeks had refused to conclude a treaty with the United States. They then followed their instructions and recommended to Knox the establishment of military posts and the raising of a military force. On January 4, 1790, Knox transmitted a report of their proceedings to President Washington and at the same time gave his own opinions regarding the Creek rejection of American offers of a treaty. He stressed that the United States would have to increase her military force should a war with the Creeks prove necessary, but after outlining his proposals in this regard he once again referred to the necessity of a change in the American attitude towards the Indians. He particularly stressed the desirability of presents and pointed out that this had always been the custom of civilized nations towards the "barbarous." "A comparative view of the expenses of a hostile or conciliatory system towards the Indians," wrote Knox, "will evince the infinite economy of the latter over the former."

Knox, even in this report which was outlining the strong possibility of military measures against the Indians, attacked the previous policy of the American government. He spoke of the policy since 1783 having resulted from "the impulses of the moment" and observed that until the Treaty of Fort Harmar in 1789 the prevailing opinion had seemed to be that the

United States had received from Great Britain not the right of pre-emption, but an absolute right to Indian territory. However, he argued, beginning with instructions in July 1788 that Indian rights should be extinguished by purchase, the United States had apparently conceded the right of soil to the Indians. Knox thought this to be a most desirable step and now said that some regular system should be established on this subject. The Indians, Knox argued, possessed "the natural rights of man" and "were these rights ascertained and declared by law; were it enacted that the Indians possess the right to all their territory which they have not fairly conveyed, and that they should not be divested thereof, but in consequence of open treaties, made under the authority of the United States, the foundation of peace and justice would be laid." [7]

Knox's hopes that peace could be established by a unified national policy were given a severe shock during 1789-1790. The winter began auspiciously in November when North Carolina at last became a member of the Union and in December ceded her western claims to the United States. However, in May 1790 the United States established the "Territory south of the River Ohio" and Washington appointed William Blount as its first governor. The appointment of this large-scale land speculator was hardly conducive to peaceful Indian relations and hardly in keeping with the new determination of the government to deal fairly with the Indians of the southwest. As superintendent of Indian affairs in the southern district Blount was to show more interest in land than in peace.[8] Also in December 1789, while North Carolina ceded her land claims to the United States, Georgia further complicated the incredible muddle of southern Indian affairs when she ceded large areas of present-day Alabama and Mississippi to three land companies. This reversed the trend of ceding land claims to the federal government and gave the Indians fresh cause for grievance.[9]

The federal government had not the slightest desire to engage in war with the southern Indians. It had become increasingly obvious that campaigns would have to be fought to ensure settlement of the available northwestern lands, and it seemed essential to avoid the dispersal of American forces that a general southern Indian war would necessitate. In view of this, and intent on exploring every avenue which might produce peace, Washington decided in the spring of 1790 to reopen negotiations with the southern Indians and in April Marinus Willett was sent as a special envoy to the Creeks. Willett visited McGillivray, gave him Washington's promises of justice, and persuaded him to visit New York to negotiate a treaty with the United States.[10]

McGillivray's visit to New York at last produced an agreement between the United States and the Creek nation. Henry Knox conducted the negotiations for the United States and showed himself willing to compromise in order to assure peace. The treaty was signed on August 7, 1790, and in it the Creeks won back some of the land forced from them by Georgia in the 1780's. The land south of the Altamaha River, which had been ceded to Georgia by the Galphinton Treaty, was now returned to the Creeks. McGillivray did not win back the land ceded by the Creeks at Augusta (the land between the Tugalo and the Apalachee rivers), for Georgians were already settled on it, but in compensation the Creeks were granted an annuity of fifteen hundred dollars. The United States also guaranteed the Creeks all their lands within the limits of the United States to the west and south of the boundary described in the treaty. In further provisions the United States promised to punish Americans who violated the Creek boundaries and provided for a maximum of four interpreters who would reside in the Creek nation to assist them in attaining "a greater degree of civilization." For the same purpose the United States promised to give the Creeks domestic animals and agricultural tools. In secret articles attached to the main treaty McGillivray was made an honorary brigadier general and promised twelve hundred dollars a year.[11] The treaty of New York was denounced in Georgia as a violation of states' rights. Western land speculators looked upon it with particular abhorrence, and the state, by its attacks on the federal treaty, encouraged its citizens to violate the boundary which had just been guaranteed by the United States Government. The United States had, in fact, promised what it could not enforce.[12]

However, having concluded an agreement with the Creeks, Washington turned to the equally serious problems of the Cherokees. Knox had already written in July 1789 that the Hopewell Treaty of November 1785 had been entirely disregarded by southern frontiersmen, and on August 11, 1790, the President informed the Senate that, as North Carolina had now joined the Union and ceded her western lands, he intended to act in regard to the violations of the agreement with the Cherokees. He asked the Senate for the authority to either enforce the Hopewell Treaty or arrange other treaties to extend the boundary to encompass the settlers. The Senate gave the President the power to act as necessary.[13]

Whether desiring peace or not, the federal government had little choice but to press as soon as possible for a land cession from the Cherokees. The Confederation's inability to enforce the Treaty of Hopewell had meant that settlers had already thrust well beyond the boundaries agreed on in 1785. Blount was ordered to arrange a new treaty with the Cherokees, but quickly showed his own inclinations by suggesting to the Secretary of War in the spring of 1791 that the cessions should be more extensive than the government had contemplated. Knox did not agree with this idea, nor did the Indians, and when in July 1791 Blount succeeded in signing the Treaty of Holston with the Cherokees, he did not obtain all he wanted. He finally had to settle for the cession of land southeast of the Clinch River (straddling what is now the Tennessee-North Carolina boundary), Cherokee agreement to a road between what is now eastern Tennessee (the Washington District) to the settlements on the Cumberland (the Mero District), and Cherokee concession of American navigation of the Tennessee River. In return the United States agreed to give one thousand dollars annually to the Cherokee nation, and it was stated that "the United States solemnly guarantee to the Cherokee nation, all their lands not hereby ceded." Moreover, by Article VIII the Cherokees were empowered to punish United States citizens who settled on their lands, and by Article XIV the United States agreed to help the Cherokee become "Herdsmen and cultivators." To this end the United States would from time to time furnish the Cherokees with "implements of husbandry" and would send not more than four persons to act as interpreters and aid the Cherokee in cultivation.[14]

In effect, though the central government had complained constantly since 1785 of the violations of the Hopewell Treaty, the unofficial advance of the settlers had now been given official sanction. Many of the settlers who had advanced into Cherokee country against federal protests, now found that the federal government had extended the boundary to include them, and those who were left in Indian country by the new line were soon to exert pressure for further cessions.

The Treaty of Holston was ratified by the Senate in November 1791, but a month later a party of Cherokees arrived in Philadelphia to express a number of objections to the treaty they had made during the summer. The main requests of the Indians were that they be given more money for the land they had ceded, that the settlers south of the ridge separating the waters of the Tennessee from those of Little River be removed, that the projected settlement at Muscle Shoals be prevented (Blount had exceeded his instructions in trying to obtain this area at the Holston treaty), and that an agent be appointed to reside in the Cherokee nation.[15]

Though Blount later said that if he had known about it the Indians would not have visited Philadelphia at all, Henry Knox showed a sympathy for the Indian point of view. On his recommendation the Senate modified the Treaty of Holston, and by an additional article in February 1792 it was agreed that the Cherokees would be paid fifteen hundred dollars instead of one thousand annually for their cession of lands. Knox also urged upon the President the necessity of removing illegal settlers from Indian lands and the blocking of any illegal settlement at Muscle Shoals.[16]

But for all the assertions of the federal government, the Creeks and Cherokees were not pacified by the actions of 1789 to 1792. The pressure of the Georgians and North Carolinians continued in spite of the Treaties of New York and Holston. Even had the frontiersmen wished to strictly observe the new boundaries, it would not have been easy. Not until the Trade and Intercourse Act of May 1796 was the white-Indian boundary carefully specified, and it was the summer of 1797 before the boundary line of the Holston Treaty of 1791 was finally marked. The federal government had continuous difficulties along the Creek and Cherokee borders.

The Choctaws and Chickasaws proved less of a problem. The President issued a proclamation in late August 1790 warning United States citizens to abide by the January 1786 Hopewell Treaties with these tribes, but this was a proclamation requiring little enforcement.[17] The lands of the Choctaws and Chickasaws were not yet in the path of the main frontier advance, and their relations with the United States were comparatively good. In fact, Chickasaw warriors accompanied Arthur St. Clair on his expedition against the northwest tribes in 1791. This use of the Chickasaws seemed so desirable to the United States Government that in 1792 the Secretary of War urged Governor Blount to secure the support of all the southern tribes for another military expedition in the Old Northwest. Knox argued that the use of southern warriors was a necessity; they had warlike propensities and would fight for the Indians if not for the Americans. But for all the talk of warlike inclinations, it seemed more likely that after St. Clair's crushing defeat the previous November the United States badly needed help in the Old Northwest.[18]

Though the United States had in 1790 and 1791 attempted to ease tension with the Creeks and Cherokees by means of moderate treaties, the next five years showed quite clearly that there was no simple solution to the problem of Indian hostilities. Relations with the Choctaws and Chickasaws remained good, but the United States now endured sporadic warfare along her southern frontiers. The Creeks in this period looked to Spain for support and bitterly resented the increasing pressure of the Georgia frontier. Some of the Cherokees remained peaceful, but the five lower towns (the Chickamaugas) put up a harsh resistance. The focal point for the attacks were the American settlements along the Cumberland River; both Creeks and Cherokees bitterly resented these settlers and made every effort to drive them out. The struggle was hopeless, for by the spring of 1794 the settlers of this area (which had been formed into the Mero District) were estimated to number some fifteen thousand. The Creeks and Cherokees had ample reason for hostility. They disliked the boundaries established at New York and Holston and even those boundaries were not observed. Though Knox and Washington had talked of the necessity of strictly honoring all treaties with the Indians and of maintaining inviolate boundary lines, the federal government proved incapable of carrying out its desires. All available federal forces were needed in the Northwest, and federal policy had to depend on solemn admonitions delivered to the southern representatives of government. With Blount as governor it could hardly be expected that the territory south of the Ohio River would strictly observe Indian boundary lines. The states of Georgia and North Carolina resented Indian occupation of their western areas and showed no disposition to regulate their citizens in an attempt to prevent incitement of the Indians. Though its assertions were more noble, the new federal government was doing little better than the Confederation in enforcing its southern Indian policy.[19]

The spring of 1792 brought sad reports of Indian depredations in the Mero District, and the federal government showed no enthusiasm for a policy of force. "It is the most ardent desire of the President of the United States, and the general government," Knox wrote to Governor Blount on April 22, "that a firm peace should be established with all the neighbouring tribes of Indians on such pure principles of justice and moderation, as will enforce the approbation of the dispassionate and enlightened part of mankind." The Secretary of War was also quite realistic in his estimate of the reason for Indian hostility—"The Indians have constantly had their jealousies and hatred excited by the attempts to obtain their lands"—but he displayed less than the supreme confidence expected of a Secretary of War when he stated that "I hope in God that all such designs are suspended for a long period." Knox showed an almost pathetic faith that good intentions on the part of the government would lead to peace and friendship on the part of the Indians. He spoke of the United States having "the fairest motives towards their happiness and interest in all respects" and asserted that "a little perseverance in such a system will teach the Indians to love and reverence the power which protects and cherishes them. The reproach which our country has sustained will be obliterated and the protection of the helpless ignorant Indians, while they demean themselves peaceably, will adorn the character of the United States." [20]

While Knox dreamed of better things, the southern frontier was the scene of continued frontier advance, sporadic warfare, and bloodshed. On July 28 Knox well demonstrated the inadequacies of even those treaties which had been signed when he told the President that Little Turkey, "the most influential chief of the Cherokees," was unhappy at the line in the vicinity of the Cumberland River and that the chief had been at neither the Treaty of Hopewell nor that at Holston. Knox feared war in the South and felt that the mass of citizens in the middle and eastern states would consider it "an insupportable evil." He implored Blount in the middle of August to do everything possible to avoid war and argued that if it did occur then "it ought to be made to appear to all the world that the government or citizens of the United States have not been the cause of bringing it on." Governor Blount was quite willing to assure the Secretary of War that the Indians had no cause of complaint. He asserted in September 1792 (when it was believed, falsely, that the Chickamaugas had entered on formal war against the United States) that the Cherokees had never complained to him of a single infraction of the Treaty of Holston and that he did not know of any such violation by a citizen of the United States.[21]

Fears that the Chickamaugas were entering into formal, all-out war against the United States proved false, but tension continued. The winter, as usual, was quieter, but in the spring of 1793 fears of war once again began to grow. The hostilities disturbed even Knox's usually sanguine opinions of the likelihood of success for the American policy. He asserted on June 26 (in a letter to Governor Blount) that "it really seems as if no permanent arrangement of peace could be made with the Savage tribes liable as they are to the impulses of bad men, and to other policy than that of the United States." Blount, of course, had been helping Knox reach this decision by his constant reports of Indian hostility and accounts of their basic opposition to the United States. On August 1, 1793, he joined with Andrew Pickens in reporting to the Secretary of War that at least the Creeks, if not the Cherokees, would have to be chastised by a military expedition before they would cease killing and robbing American frontier settlers. They also warned that the Chickasaws and Choctaws would become enemies of the United States if they continued to trade entirely with the Spanish. The same pattern continued throughout the summer and into the fall. Blount urged the necessity for firm action against the Creeks and Cherokees while Knox tried to restrain the frontier settlers who were crossing the lines established earlier in the decade.[22]

The main thrust of Indian resistance was still directed against the settlements in the Mero District along the Cumberland River, and as hostility continued, increasing southwestern pressure was exerted on Knox for a more active and militant federal policy. Knox, however, reported to the President in April 1794 that the inhabitants of the Mero District would have to depend on local militia for their defense, and at the end of May Congress authorized the President to call out the militia to take the offensive against the Creeks and Cherokees when it was necessary. Congress also authorized the establishment of military posts.[23]

Fortunately for Knox, in the early summer of 1794 the Cherokees at last appeared somewhat less warlike. Knox had long urged that a Cherokee delegation be persuaded to visit Philadelphia to arrange a settlement, and in the early summer of 1794 a party travelled to the federal capital. While at Philadelphia the Cherokees signed a treaty confirming the Treaty of Holston, and in return their annuity was increased from fifteen hundred dollars to five thousand.[24] But though the Indians were happy to receive an increased annuity, their basic grievances were not assuaged. Raids continued on the Mero settlements, and in September an unauthorized expedition from the Mero District raided the Lower Cherokee towns. By November, however, hopes of settlement with the Cherokees were renewed, and at Tellico Blockhouse a delegation of Cherokees assured Blount of their peaceful intentions. Toward the Creeks, however, he envisaged no policy but war. "If the Citizens of the United States, do not destroy the Creeks," wrote Blount on November 10, 1794, "the Creeks will kill the Citizens of the United States, the alternative is to kill or be killed." Later that month he requested authority to use the Cherokees, Chickasaws, and Choctaws to attack the Creeks.[25]

While Blount bewailed the hostility of the Creeks, the state of Georgia demonstrated why the Creeks were so bitter. In December 1794 the Georgia Assembly appropriated lands for the payment of state troops, lands which had been guaranteed to the Creeks by the federal government in the Treaty of New York and were claimed by Georgia not on the basis of federal negotiations but because of the Georgia-Indian treaties of the 1780's. Georgia urged the federal government to negotiate another treaty of cession if the Indians refused to accept this latest claim. Moreover, in January 1795 great areas of land were granted to land companies in the Southwest in the famous "Yazoo Fraud"—and this at a time when the Creeks were already infuriated by the policies of the previous ten years.[26]

Georgia thus pressed on regardless of threats of war, Indian resistance, or governmental policies. Blount continued advocating war against the Creeks as the only method of achieving peace, although Knox kept urging the avoidance of hostilities. In March 1795 he wrote a long letter to Blount essentially opposing the policies of both the governor and Georgia. He told him that Congress had appropriated fifty thousand dollars for opening a trade with the Indians and one hundred and forty thousand dollars for the defense of the frontiers. "All ideas of offensive operations are therefore to be laid aside," wrote Knox, "and all possible harmony cultivated with the Indian Tribes." After emphasizing his belief that tranquillity was once again arriving on the southern frontiers, he expressed a polite mistrust of Blount. "Upon the whole, Sir," Knox stated, "I cannot refrain from saying that the complexion of some of the Transactions in the South western territory appears unfavourable to the public interests." He also expressed the opinion that there would not be tranquillity on the frontiers as long as American settlers encroached on Indian lands. While his desire to prevent encroachment was praiseworthy, the ultimate problem was of course the original cession of lands and the prospect of further cessions.[27]

This became readily apparent in June 1795 when, in spite of Knox's analysis of the causes of Indian hostility, President Washington acted in response to Georgia's demands of the previous December. On June 25 the President submitted to the Senate the names of Benjamin Hawkins, George Clymer, and Andrew Pickens as commissioners for a treaty with the Creeks. Once again the Creeks were to be asked to relinquish lands, and in the spring of 1796 they were summoned to Colerain on the St. Mary's River for a negotiation. The Creeks had to contend not only with the commissioners of the United States, but also with commissioners from Georgia who had been invited by the federal government to safeguard the interests of the state. In this they were disappointed, for the Creeks objected bitterly to Georgia's demands for land, and the federal commissioners would not compel the Creeks to yield. On June 29, 1796, the Treaty of Colerain was signed. In essence, it confirmed the Treaty of New York and defined the boundaries established at that time. The Georgia Commissioners were furious and on the day before the treaty was signed issued an official protest. They bitterly complained of the relinquishment of land to the Creeks (particularly the land which had been appropriated for the payment of state troops) and objected to the restrictions that had been placed on them in the treaty camp in regard to meeting with the Indians. Moreover, the Georgia commissioners objected to the fact that the United States Commissioners had stated in council that the Georgia-Creek Treaties of Augusta, Galphinton, and Shoulderbone were invalid, and they protested the Creek cessions of small tracts of land to the United States for posts within the territorial limits of Georgia. Though the United States had been persuaded to negotiate this treaty by the pressures of the state of Georgia, it had only led to further bitterness between the federal government and the state. The Creeks had emerged reasonably successful from the negotiations. They had resisted demands for further substantial cessions of land and had received six thousand dollars for the two small tracts they had ceded on the Altamaha and Oconee rivers for posts.[28]

Though there was comparative peace along the Creek frontier, dangers of further outbreaks were increasing along the Cherokee borders. The immediate problem was that the boundary line decided upon at the Treaty of Holston in 1791 had not yet been run and was already out of date. Settlers were illegally established on land that the Cherokees had been allowed to keep in 1791, and encroachment was increasing rapidly. When the boundary was finally marked in 1797, the federal government was again placed in the embarrassing position of either having to remove its citizens from Indian land or negotiate for more land. On federal orders settlers withdrew from the Indian side of the line; this quickly led to protests from the state of Tennessee which had entered the Union in 1796.[29] President John Adams heeded the protests of the new state, and in March 1798 Secretary of War James McHenry sent instructions to Commissioners Alfred Moore, George Walton, and John Steel to negotiate with the Cherokees.

"A primary consideration," wrote the Secretary of War, "will be, to dispose the minds of the Cherokees to make a sale of such part of their land as will give a more convenient form to the State of Tennessee, and conduce to the protection of its citizens." In particular the commissioners were to negotiate for the cession of those lands on the fringes of the boundaries that had been owned by American settlers until they had been removed by the federal government after the official drawing of the Holston boundary in 1797. Once again the Indians felt the pressure of American demands, and on October 2, 1798, at Tellico, Tennessee, after preliminary resistance early in the summer, the Cherokees agreed to cede three separate tracts—one between the Clinch River and the Cumberland Mountains and two south of the Holston cession of 1791. For this they received five thousand dollars in goods and an additional one thousand dollars in their annuity. They also received the promise that the United States "will continue the guarantee of the remainder of their country, forever, as contained in former treaties." [30]

In the first decade of its existence the federal government had certainly tried to bring some order into the chaos of southern Indian affairs. These attempts had involved determined efforts to restrain the frontiersmen of Georgia, North Carolina, and Tennessee. Georgia had been infuriated by the New York and Colerain Treaties with the Creeks, for in those treaties the federal government had given back to the Creeks land that Georgia had obtained by cession from parts of that tribe during the 1780's. Though the Treaty of Holston with the Cherokees in 1791 less flagrantly opposed the position of the southern states, American settlers in the following years pushed up to and across the agreed boundary. Moreover, in spite of the federal effort to enforce firm boundaries, the Creeks and Cherokees engaged in sporadic warfare on frontier settlements throughout these first years of the new national government. These Indians still resented the loss of the lands they had yielded in the years since the Revolution and were no more entranced by the planned advance contemplated by the federal government than they were by the disordered advance of the southern frontiersmen.

Yet, the federal government still had great hopes that firmly established boundaries, an orderly advance, and the bringing of civilization would produce peace. When, in the spring of 1799, Thomas Lewis replaced Silas Dinsmoor as agent to the Cherokees, his instructions reflected the continuing governmental hopes. He was told that it had been a principal object of the labors of his predecessor to introduce spinning and weaving among the Cherokee women and agriculture and stock raising among the men. Lewis was to continue this policy and for this "plan of civilization" was advanced four hundred dollars. He was also to protect the boundaries of the Cherokee country from potential settlers.[31] As the first decade of federal relations with the southern Indians came to an end, the federal government placed its greatest hopes in its policy of bringing civilization to the Indians. That the effort expended on this policy was comparatively small and that the majority of Indians east of the Mississippi were as yet unaffected by it, in no regard dimmed the enthusiasm of those who hoped that it would prove the key both to successful and peaceful American expansion and to the maintenance of the good character of the nation.

The Old Northwest, 1789—1795

VI

I N THE OLD NORTHWEST as in the South the federal government found it no simple matter to undo the Indian policies of the Confederation. Though the spring and summer of 1789 brought federal statements of the necessity of a new compromise policy, the tribes along the Wabash were showing increased hostility to American settlers. The settlements in Kentucky were particularly hard-hit by Indian attacks, and in August 1789 the Kentuckians sent an unauthorized and ineffective expedition into the Indian country.[1] It was obvious that the complaints of the frontiersmen would force the federal government to take some positive action, and on September 29, 1789, Congress empowered the President to call out state militia to protect the frontiers from hostile Indians. Early in October Washington wrote to Governor Arthur St. Clair of the Northwest Territory authorizing him to call out the militia of Virginia and Pennsylvania if he could not secure peace with the Indians of the Wabash and Illinois. He asserted, however, that "a war with the Wabash Indians ought to be avoided by all means consistently with the security of the frontier inhabitants, the security of the troops, and the national dignity." Yet, he argued, if the Indians refused offers of peace, it would be necessary to punish them. This alternative of war was not relished by the United States, and in December Secretary of War Knox reiterated to St. Clair the President's desire that all possible efforts be made to secure a peace treaty with the Wabash Indians.[2]

In the winter of 1789-1790 St. Clair made an attempt to carry out his instructions from Washington and Knox. He travelled deep into the Old Northwest reaching Vincennes at the beginning of January 1790 and leaving shortly afterwards for the Illinois country. While travelling he sent other agents to the Wabash tribes. His travels and messages produced little result, and on May 1 he wrote to both Washington and Knox that he feared that the United States would have to chastise the northwest Indians.[3]

St. Clair's warnings were hardly needed in the East, where news of Indian depredations along the Ohio had already made it seem extremely unlikely that war could be avoided. On May 27 Knox suggested in a report to the President that an expedition was needed northwest of the Ohio. Optimistically, he considered that the hostilities were the action of a minority of "banditti" Indians and that a force of some one hundred regulars and three hundred militia would be sufficient for the expedition. Knox also wrote to Josiah Harmar, commander of American forces along the Ohio, and to St. Clair asking them to discuss the best method of extirpating the hostile group of Indians beyond the Ohio, though he stressed that this should not interfere with the plans for a general accommodation "with the regular tribes." It was typical of Knox's optimism, and blindness to the real attitude of the Indians, that he believed Indian hostilities were merely the work of a small group and did not represent any general resentment on the part of the Indian nations.[4]

St. Clair's visit to Vincennes and the Illinois country had given him no reason to believe that peace could be secured, and in July he returned east to Fort Washington (the site of Cincinnati) to confer with Harmar. These northwestern leaders did not have Knox's optimism concerning the extent of Indian resistance and decided upon a larger operation than Knox had envisaged. While a fairly small force would proceed from Vincennes against the Indian villages along the Wabash, Harmar would lead some three hundred regulars and twelve hundred militia from Fort Washington to the Indian villages at the portage between the Maumee and the Wabash (later the site of Fort Wayne). It was hoped that both these expeditions would begin about October 1.[5] Knox was rapidly discovering that in spite of government assertions of a new and more benign Indian policy, there was an immediate necessity for extensive military operations in the Old Northwest.

On August 23, 1790, Knox, on behalf of the President, approved the plans that had been suggested by St. Clair and Harmar and on September 12 stated the objects of the campaign: "The proposed expedition is intended to exhibit to the Wabash Indians our power to punish them for their hostile depredations, for their conniving at the depredations of others, and for their refusing to treat with the United States when invited thereto."[6] The Indians were fighting to resist pressure on their lands, and treaties with the American government almost invariably resulted in the confirmation of cessions or demands for new ones; yet when the Indians refused to negotiate, this was used as a reason for a military expedition. Though Knox had asserted that the Indians held the right of soil and could choose whether or not to sell their lands, this concept of free choice broke down under the pressure of the frontier advance.

The hopes that a display of force would induce the Indians to keep the peace and enter into negotiations with the Americans soon collapsed. The western wing of the attack into the Indian country proceeded ineffectually from Vincennes along the Wabash at the end of September. The Indians avoided contact with the small American force, and it accomplished practically nothing.[7] Harmar, who had left Fort Washington with his force of over fourteen hundred men just a few days before the sortie from Vincennes, had equal difficulty in bringing the Indians to battle when and where he desired. In the middle of October he reached the Indian villages in the region of what is now Fort Wayne, Indiana. Though he burned them, he was unable to engage the main Indian force, and American hopes were completely frustrated when detached parties of Harmar's force were defeated in two separate engagements. Knox had little reason for rejoicing when Harmar arrived back at Fort Washington early in November 1790.[8]

In the winter Knox planned the next steps that would safely enable American settlers to occupy lands northwest of the Ohio River. In a report to the President on January 22, 1791, he suggested that another expedition was needed against the Wabash Indians and that its object should be to establish a post in the heart of the Indian country, at the portage of the Maumee and the Wabash. His estimates of the force required for a new expedition had risen sharply, for he now thought that three thousand men would be needed to bring it to success.[9] At the beginning of March 1791 Congress authorized the increase of the regular army to that number. While the large expedition was being prepared, it was decided that small sorties should be used to divert Indian hostility from the American frontiers.[10]

In another attempt to divert the extensive Indian attacks that could be expected in the spring and summer, Colonel Thomas Procter was sent as envoy to the Indians along the Maumee and Wabash. He was to try to convince these hostile tribes of the justice and candor of the United States Government and persuade them to come to Fort Washington for treaty negotiations. The mission was a complete fiasco. Procter hoped to travel on Lake Erie, but when he reached Niagara discovered that the British commander would not give him permission to take that route. (The British retention of the northwest posts enabled them to rule the lakes.) Procter also

encountered difficulties from the lack of order in governmental policy, for though he had been ordered to enlist
friendly chiefs of the Six Nations to accompany him on a
peace mission to the Wabash Indians, he found that while he
was there St. Clair sent a request to the Six Nations for warriors to fight with the Americans on their expedition into the
Northwest. Eventually, the Six Nations heeded yet another
request of the American government—to meet in council in
the spring and cement American-Six Nations friendship. Thus
in June Procter gave up his attempt to proceed west of
Niagara and returned to Philadelphia.[11]

Procter's mission had always seemed doomed to failure, and
in the spring and summer of 1791 the government hastened its
military preparations. Two diversionary attacks on Wabash
towns by expeditions from Kentucky in May and August had
no real effect on Indian resistance, and all depended on the
major expedition which was to leave from Fort Washington.[12]
After Harmar's failure of the previous year, this expedition
was now entrusted to the governor of the Northwest Territory, Arthur St. Clair. St. Clair's instructions were sent to him
on March 21, 1791. He was told that the United States did not
desire war—the expense would far exceed the advantages to be
gained from it—but that if peace measures failed there was no
alternative. For all this talk of the undesirability of war, Knox
made it obvious that the United States stood to gain consid-
erably from a military victory. St. Clair was told that "in order
to avoid future wars" it might be proper to push the Indians
back beyond the line formed by the Maumee and the Wabash.
As long as the Wyandots and Delawares remained friendly,
they could be exempted from this boundary, but if they joined
the hostile Indians then they too should be pushed back. Knox
also suggested that St. Clair judge whether or not it would be
proper to extend the boundary westwards from the mouth of
Wildcat Creek on the Wabash due west to the Mississippi.[13]

Though Knox had repeatedly stated that the land-grabbing
of the 1780's had been misguided and had urged a policy of
moderation as a means of winning Indian friendship and

preserving national honor, he was now suggesting that a military expedition, which had been entered into reluctantly, should be used to obtain the cession of a whole vast new area of land in the Old Northwest. Instead of eastern and southern Ohio, this boundary would have meant that the Indians would cede practically all of present-day Ohio and much of Indiana and Illinois. With one blow the United States hoped to obtain title all the way west to the Mississippi River, though the Indians had been protesting the treaties of the 1780's because the American settlements had been pushed beyond the Ohio.

The expedition of St. Clair was to realize none of these hopes. Slowly, through the spring and summer of 1791, St. Clair prepared to attack. He had difficulties obtaining suitable supplies and men, and it was not until early in October that his main army began to move north. On November 3, some one hundred miles north of Fort Washington, the American force was overwhelmed by a sudden Indian attack. Over six hundred were killed, and the rest fled in confusion back to Fort Washington. American hopes of establishing safe settlements beyond the Ohio (and possibly extending American boundaries to the Mississippi) had been dealt a crushing blow.[14]

Even more in the North than in the South the American government was discovering that the establishment of satisfactory relations with the Indians demanded more than expressions of good will. On December 26, 1791, Knox again reported to the President on the subject of the northwest frontiers. He stated what was now obvious, that the Indians would have to be convinced of the superior force of the Americans before they would be prepared to make peace. He defended American military action on the grounds that it was a just war, asked for another attempt to establish a fort at the portage of the Maumee and the Wabash, and now suggested an army of over five thousand men.[15] In his "Statement of Causes of the Indian War," which was prepared at the President's request and dated January 26, 1792, Knox continued

his justification of this war in the Old Northwest. He emphasized that at Fort Harmar in 1789 the United States had purchased from the Indians the lands that had previously been
forced from the Indians in treaties between 1784 and 1786. He
said that the present war seemed to have arisen not from
disputes concerning the boundaries established at those treaties, but from the unprovoked aggressions of the Miami and
Wabash Indians.[16]

By the beginning of 1792 American Indian policy in the
Old Northwest had been a disastrous failure. After 1789 the
government had asserted its desire for a policy of peace and
conciliation, had discovered that the Indians did not want to
cede land either by war or purchase, and had been forced
into two most inglorious military expeditions. Another expedition was obviously needed, but it was essential that it should
not be a failure. To attempt to ensure this, careful preparation was needed, and careful preparation would take time.
There was a great danger that while an expedition was prepared, the Indians would ravage the American frontier settlements. Accordingly, in 1792 and 1793, the United States sent a
series of peace missions to the northwest Indians making every
effort to convince them of the good intentions of the American
government and offering concessions in the hope that this
would maintain peace and protect the American frontier
settlements.

The first of these peace efforts, early in 1792, met with the
same fate as Thomas Procter's in the previous year. On January 9, 1792, Knox sent instructions to Captain Peter Pond
and William Steedman. "No doubt can exist that our strength
and our resources are abundant to conquer, and even extirpate the Indians, northwest of the Ohio," wrote Knox, "But
this is not our object. We wish to be at peace with those
Indians—to be their friends and protectors—to perpetuate
them on the land." This statement can only be understood in
terms of Knox's hopes for the bringing of civilization and
private property to the Indians. It had been made quite obvious in the Northwest Ordinance of 1787 and in the instruc-

tions to St. Clair in March 1791 that the United States intended to expand across the Old Northwest to the Mississippi River. In view of this, the only way that the Indians could be perpetuated on the land would be as farmers in the midst of the American advance. In effect, Pond and Steedman were given impossible instructions, for they were told by Knox that the United States could not ask the Indians to make peace, as they were considered the aggressors, but the envoys should persuade the Indians to sue for peace from the United States. How this was to be accomplished, in view of the great victory won by the Indians over St. Clair, is difficult to imagine, but as it turned out Pond and Steedman could not even persuade the British to let them travel on Lake Erie, and they had to turn back.[17]

The government also attempted to use the chiefs of the Six Nations to win the friendship of the western Indians. The Six Nations had been engulfed by the advance of the American frontier, and though Joseph Brant and his Mohawks were trying from Canada to organize resistance to the American frontier advance, the Six Nations within American territory were in no position to present real opposition. At a council in June and July, 1791, the Six Nations, who had already ceded their claims to the land northwest of the Ohio desired by the United States, were guaranteed the territory on which they lived. As the lands left to the Six Nations within the United States were all within the bounds of existing states, the federal government was hardly making any great concession.[18]

As an aftermath of this conference some of the Iroquois chiefs visited Philadelphia in March 1792. While they were there the Senate agreed to appropriate fifteen hundred dollars annually to help towards the civilization of the Six Nations, and some of their chiefs were persuaded to travel west to tell the hostile Indians of the American desire for peace. It was not until the fall of 1792 that they attempted to carry out their mission, and by that time their failure was only one of several others.[19] Not only were these friendly chiefs of the Six Nations sent into the West, but two other Indians were dispatched separately in the summer of 1792. In May Knox instructed Captain Hendrick Aupaumut of the Stockbridge Indians to tell the western Indians that the United States wanted no lands but those obtained in fair treaty, and in June Joseph Brant was hopefully sent on the same mission. The influential Brant had listened far more to the British than to the Americans and had led Indian resistance against them in the late 1780's, but the Americans now made great efforts to secure him for their cause. Though Brant rejected the one thousand guinea reward for working towards peace, he did agree to visit the western Indians. Knox instructed Brant, like Aupaumut, to inform the western Indians that the United States wanted only land obtained in fair treaty.[20] In the summer and fall of 1792, while the harassed United States began preparations for another expedition into the Old Northwest, the chiefs of the Six Nations, Captain Hendrick Aupaumut, and Joseph Brant all travelled west to promise the western Indians that the United States would not take their lands by force.

While the Indian emissaries were being feted in Philadelphia and prepared for their mission to the West, the United States, acting on the scattergun principle, sent out two more peace expeditions. On April 3, 1792, Knox issued instructions to Captain Alexander Trueman. He was to proceed to the villages at the Maumee-Wabash portage and persuade the Indians to come into Philadelphia for treaty discussions. The message Knox sent to the western Indians said that the United States did not want to deprive them of their lands, but wanted to teach them the blessings of civilized life. Instructions were also sent to Colonel John Hardin on May 20, 1792, to visit the tribes on the Sandusky River to either persuade them to visit Philadelphia or at least arrange a joint conference in the West with the Indians who were being visited by Trueman. In such a conference the Indians could be told of the American desire for peace. This peace mission was particularly disastrous, for both Trueman and Hardin were killed by hostile Indians.[21]

The most important envoy of 1792 received his instructions on May 22. Brigadier General Rufus Putnam was to try to attend the general council of hostile Indians soon to be held on the Maumee and convince them of the good intentions of the United States. He was given authority to renounce *"in the strongest and most explicit terms"* all claims to Indian land which had not already been ceded "by fair treaties." Moreover, he could relinquish tracts of land which had been ceded for United States posts within the Indian boundaries, with the exception of the land around Detroit. "You will make it clearly understood," wrote Knox, "that we want not a foot of their land, and that it is theirs, and theirs only—That they have the right to sell, and the right to refuse to sell, and that the United States will guarantee to them their said just rights." Putnam was to tell the tribes that a new government had been formed in the United States, with Washington at its head, and that "in future, all the Indian Nations may rest with great confidence upon the justice, the humanity, and the liberality, of the United States." Knox again stressed that the United States was anxious to impart to the Indians "the blessings of civilization."

Knox concluded his instructions to Putnam by asserting that his first object was to convince the Indians that the United States required none of their land. His second object should be to assure them that the United States would guarantee all the land that remained and take the Indians under United States protection, providing that the Indians would conclude an immediate truce.[22]

Putnam travelled west in June, but he decided to avoid the Maumee when he heard of the deaths of Trueman and Hardin. Instead, he proceeded to Vincennes. In August Knox approved this change in plans, again repeating that "The United States require no lands of the Wabash indians not heretofore ceded," and Putnam finally arrived at Vincennes in mid-September.[23] There he held a council with a number of the Wabash tribes, and after he had assured the Indians that the United States wanted no more of their lands, a treaty was signed on September 27. It was a short treaty, and it reflected the American defeats of the early 1790's. After stating that there would be peace between the United States and the Wabash and Illinois Indians, the treaty was explicit on the subject of Indian lands: "The United States solemnly guarantee to the Wabash, and the Illinois nations, or tribes of Indians, all the lands to which they have a just claim; and no part shall ever be taken from them, but by a fair purchase, and to their satisfaction. That the lands originally belonged to the Indians; it is theirs, and theirs only. That they have a right to sell, and a right to refuse to sell. And that the United States will protect them in their said just rights." [24] This solemn guarantee contrasts strangely to the instructions to St. Clair in March 1791, just eighteen months before, when Knox had hoped that following a military victory the United States boundaries could be extended to the Mississippi.

Even in time of crisis the terms Putnam agreed to at Vincennes proved too much for the government to swallow. If, as expected, the pressure of American settlement would eventually induce the Indians to sell their lands to the Americans, it was essential that provision be made for this by inserting into the treaty a definite United States right of pre-emption. The lack of this provision in the Vincennes Treaty caused Knox anxiety, and Washington drew the attention of the Senate to its omission when he submitted the treaty for ratification in February 1793. After long delay the Senate, early in 1794, voted against ratification of the treaty.[25] However, American withdrawal from this agreement was less disastrous than it might have been, for the Wabash Indians themselves were by that time violating the peace.

Putnam had avoided the Maumee, but other envoys of the United States did travel there to the Indian gathering in the fall. These envoys, though, were Indian messengers of the United States, and their journeys were of no avail. Brant did not even reach the council until it was over, and the other Indian messengers were told that the Indians desired an Ohio River boundary and would meet the Americans in the following spring to discuss a settlement.[26]

The Old Northwest, 1789–1795

By the end of 1792 the American government was in dire trouble in the Old Northwest. It was essential that lands beyond the Ohio be made available for sale and settlement, but the attempt of the new federal government to uphold by military force the treaties dictated by the Confederation in the 1780's had proved a failure. Though the talk was of conciliation, concession, and the bringing of civilization, the United States could not give back the lands forced from the Indians in the 1780's. What was happening, however, was that under the pressure of military defeat the United States was perhaps going further than was wise in explicitly guaranteeing the Indians any land that they had not yet ceded. It was hoped that by giving the Indians a clear right to the land they still held that they could be persuaded to keep the peace and the land ceded in the 1780's could be settled. The guarantees meant little, for the United States had already made it obvious through the Northwest Ordinance, and a variety of assertions, that she intended to settle the land between the Ohio and the Mississippi. Neither Knox nor Washington had any real reason to think they were risking much by giving a guarantee of Indian land, for both of them had already expressed the view that a boundary line would never prove permanent as white settlement pressed up to the boundary. The Indians would either be exterminated, retire, or would easily yield land which was no longer useful to them. Yet, both Knox and Washington hoped, though they had little reason for such optimism, that the Americans could prove the benefactor rather than the exterminator of the Indians.

The United States had no choice in 1792 but to accept the hostile Indian proposal for a council the following year. At least such a council might keep the Indians quiet until the army which was to redeem the defeats of Harmar and St. Clair had been prepared for offensive warfare. Anthony Wayne had been given command of a northwest army after the defeat of St. Clair, and he was carefully arranging for yet another expedition into the heart of the hostile Indian country.

In December 1792 Knox replied to the Indian message and agreed that the United States would negotiate with them in the spring. In a letter to Anthony Wayne in January 1793 Knox asserted that it was necessary to enter into negotiation with the Indians as the majority of United States citizens were averse to an Indian war. "If the war continues," wrote Knox, "the extirpation and destruction of the Indian tribes are inevitable—This is desired to be avoided, as the honor and future reputation of the Country is more intimately blended therewith than is generally supposed." [27]

The peace conference of 1793—the most organized attempt for a settlement between the Treaties of Fort Harmar in 1789 and the Treaty of Greenville in 1795—foundered on the Indian refusal to concede lands beyond the Ohio at a time when they were undefeated in the field. The question of instructions for the American commissioners was taken up at the very highest level. On February 17 Washington informed the Secretary of State, the Secretary of the Treasury, and the Attorney General that he was going to consult them on the instructions prepared by the Secretary of War. At a meeting at the President's house on February 24 the biggest problem was deciding whether or not it was proper to empower the commissioners to recede from the existing boundary northwest of the Ohio (that gained by the treaties of the 1780's) if peace could be obtained in no other way. The Secretaries of Treasury (Alexander Hamilton), War (Knox), and the Attorney General (Edmund Randolph) all thought that this could and should be done if necessary to secure peace. Secretary of State Jefferson, however, did not agree, and even the majority stipulated that any retrocession to the Indians should not infringe upon grants to individuals or reservations to states.[28]

A distinguished commission of Benjamin Lincoln, Beverly Randolph, and Timothy Pickering was chosen to negotiate with the Indians, and their instructions were finally issued on April 26. They were told to do their utmost to obtain confirmation of the boundaries of Fort Harmar, if some tribes with claims had not been paid, then they should be paid now. In return the United States would guarantee "the right of soil, to all the remaining Indian lands in that quarter, against the citizens or inhabitants of United States." Also cessions for posts on the Indian side of the boundary obtained at Fort Harmar would be given back to the Indians, and they would be given fifty thousand dollars in goods at the treaty and ten thousand dollars annually. In essence, the United States was offering more money for the line obtained at Fort Harmar. It was, however, suggested that if the Indians insisted upon it, a slight withdrawal could be made from the Fort Harmar line to the tracts of land already granted to certain companies by the United States. It was pointed out that such a cession would cause continual friction and that there was only a very small area between the Fort Harmar boundary and the granted tracts; furthermore, it was particularly stressed that whatever the agreement, it was essential that the United States obtain the right of pre-emption.[29]

In spite of fears of lack of support for the war, the military defeats of 1790 and 1791, and the special cabinet meetings to discuss withdrawal, it was obvious that the United States still wanted what had first been demanded and then asked for since 1783: the cession of what is now eastern and southern Ohio. This was the land which for the most part had already been sold to land companies and into which American settlers were moving. In essence, the Indians would either sell this in a peaceful treaty, or they would be forced to yield it by military action. If peace could be achieved along the boundary line established with the Indian tribes between 1784 and 1786, then the American side of the boundary would rapidly fill with settlers, and future Indian cessions in the Old Northwest would be assured.

The United States Commissioners arrived at the Detroit River in July 1793. They never reached the Maumee to negotiate formally with the Indian tribes, for it soon became quite obvious that agreement was impossible. At the end of July an Indian deputation told the commissioners that the Ohio River should be the boundary line between the whites and the Indians. "If you seriously design to make a firm and lasting peace," the commissioners were told, "you will immediately remove all your people from our side of that river." The commissioners replied that lands north of the Ohio had been ceded by the Indians in formal treaty and that large tracts had already been sold and settled: "it is impossible to make the river Ohio the boundary, between your people and the people of the United States." After effectively killing the negotiations, the commissioners attempted to breathe life into them by retracting the position that had been maintained by the Confederation Government in the 1780's. They stated that the United States Commissioners of the 1780's had erred in asserting that the United States had obtained complete rights to all the land east of the Mississippi in 1783. These negotiators of 1793 expressly conceded that the right of soil in the area ceded by the British in 1783 was in the hands of the Indian nations "so long as they desire to occupy the same." But for all this concession of error in the 1780's, the Indians could not be won over. They suggested that the United States take the money that she was prepared to give them and use it to compensate American settlers north of the Ohio for leaving their lands and returning south of that river. The peroration of the Indian reply was an eloquent one: "We desire you to consider, brothers, that our only demand is the peaceable possession of a small part of our once great country. Look back, and review the lands from whence we have been driven to this spot. We can retreat no farther, because the country behind hardly affords food for its present inhabitants; and we have therefore resolved to leave our bones in this small space to which we are now confined." Many of them were to fulfill this resolve.[30]

The negotiations of 1793 had failed, and another expedition was now inevitable. In truth, the government had never really expected success. Jefferson wrote in November 1793 that "Our negotiations with the North-Western Indians have completely failed, so that war must settle our difference. We expected nothing else, and had gone into negotiations only to prove to all our citizens that peace was unattainable on terms which any one of them would admit." [31]

The government had hoped that the failure of negotiations in 1793 could immediately be followed by a military expedition into the Old Northwest. This proved impossible, for the negotiations dragged on much later into the summer of 1793 than had been expected. Accordingly, Anthony Wayne only advanced a limited distance north from Fort Washington in the fall of 1793 and established Fort Greenville. There he spent the winter, and it was not until the following summer that he finally advanced northward and brought the Indians to battle. Eventually, on August 20, 1794, Wayne defeated the Indians at the Battle of Fallen Timbers near the rapids of the Maumee. This victory doomed the hopes of the Indians northwest of the Ohio that, particularly given the extent of the support they were receiving from the British, they would be able to stem the American advance at the Ohio River. This hope was, of course, never realistic, and having lost the Battle of Fallen Timbers the Indians were forced to yield what they had defended since 1783.[32]

Knox had told Wayne as early as April 1794 that the boundaries of Fort Harmar could form the basis of a peace settlement in the Old Northwest, and in the winter of 1794-95 Wayne and the Indian tribes carried on preliminary discussions for a peace settlement; those tribes that signed preliminary agreements agreed to assemble at Greenville in June for the conclusion of a formal treaty.[33] The task of supplying Wayne with instructions for the treaty fell to the new Secretary of War, Timothy Pickering. On April 8, 1795, he sent these instructions to Wayne and told him that he was sending goods to the value of twenty-five thousand dollars which were to be delivered to the Indians only in the event of a successful treaty. Wayne was also empowered to grant the Indians an annuity of ten thousand dollars as a further and full consideration for the lands they relinquished. In 1791 Knox had suggested the cession of lands to the Mississippi in the event of a military victory, but several years of defeat had produced greater moderation, and Pickering stipulated that the general boundary line of the Treaty of Fort Harmar would still be satisfactory to the United States. In addition, however, he suggested that it would be desirable to retain the trading posts obtained at Fort Harmar and establish a chain of military posts to complete lines of communication from the Ohio to the Maumee, from the Miami villages (Fort Wayne) to the head of the Wabash, down the Wabash to the Ohio, and from the Miami villages along the Maumee to its mouth on Lake Erie. Yet, Pickering added, *"all* these Cessions are not to be insisted on; for *peace* and not *increase* of *territory* has been the object of this expensive War." Pickering stressed in his letter that the statement by the post-1783 commissioners that all the land to the Mississippi was "the *full* and *absolute* property of the United States" had been repeatedly renounced and was "a construction as unfounded in itself as it was unintelligible and mysterious to the Indians." The right of pre-emption, however, had to be maintained.

On April 14 Pickering added a postscript to this letter of the 8th and enclosed a copy of the treaty he desired. In most important respects this draft was identical to the treaty eventually signed by the Indians, though Wayne gained additional land and posts within the Indian territory. On April 15 Pickering again wrote to Wayne and partially explained why the United States, after Wayne's decisive victory over the Indians at Fallen Timbers, was prepared to settle for the Fort Harmar line. "When a peace shall once be established," wrote Pickering, "and we also take possession of the posts now held by the British, we can obtain every thing we shall want with a tenth part of the trouble and difficulty which you would now have to encounter." [34] This statement was certainly in accord with Pickering's earlier thinking. In June 1785, after the Treaties of Forts McIntosh and Stanwix, he had asserted that it would be a mistake to acquire any more land at that time: "The demand for what we now have would lessen in proportion to the additional acquisitions. The purchase will be as easy made at any future period as at this time. Indians having no ideas of wealth, and their numbers always lessening in the neighbourhood of our Settlements, their claims for compensation will likewise be diminished; and besides that, fewer will remain to be gratified, the game will be greatly reduced, and lands destitute of game will, by hunters, be lightly esteemed." [35] Like

Washington and Knox, Pickering had faith that there was no such thing as a permanent boundary and that the pressure of white population would ensure that the Indians would be willing to sell and sell cheaply.

Though the council had been called for the middle of June, the actual business of the Greenville Treaty did not begin until the middle of July. The proceedings lasted until August 3, but there was no negotiation in the real sense of the word. Wayne had won a military victory. The Indians knew it, and they also knew that they could not depend upon the British for support. Wayne obtained Indian approval of the treaty he had brought to the conference, and the Indians could offer no real resistance.[36]

The Greenville Treaty of August 3, 1795, gained for the United States not only the eastern and southern sections of what is now the state of Ohio, but also a strip (the gore) of what is now southeastern Indiana. Wayne had actually obtained more than Pickering had suggested (Pickering did not ask for land beyond the Great Miami) as Pickering's reiteration of his belief in a Great Miami boundary did not reach Wayne until after the treaty had been signed. The United States also obtained some sixteen separate reservations of land on the Indian side of the Greenville line; these ranged from the Sandusky River in the East to Michilimackinac in the North and to the mouth of the Illinois River in the West. The Indian tribes also granted the United States free passage by land and water between the chain of posts which had been ceded so that the United States now had a network of posts and strategic routes covering the whole Northwest. Though American settlers were not to be allowed beyond the Greenville line, the American government was ensuring that it would maintain control throughout the whole region. In return for this cession it was stated in Article IV that "the United States relinquish their claims to all other Indian lands, northward of the river Ohio, eastward of the Mississippi, and westward and southward of the Great Lakes, and the waters uniting them." The United States also paid twenty thousand dollars in goods immediately and promised ninety-five hundred dollars in goods annually.

Article V of the Greenville Treaty re-emphasized that the Indians could retain for as long as they wished the lands they had been allowed to keep, but it also stated emphatically that the United States had the right of pre-emption: "the Indian tribes who have a right to those lands, are quietly to enjoy them, hunting, planting, and dwelling thereon, so long as they please, without any molestation from the United States; but when those tribes, or any of them, shall be disposed to sell their lands, or any part of them, they are to be sold only to the United States." The remainder of the Greenville Treaty was primarily concerned with the keeping of the peace and the question of trade. There was no doubt that the United States intended to prevent frontier incidents and protect the boundary line from violation by its own citizens. This would keep the peace which was essential to the safe and rapid settlement of those areas that had now been ceded by the Indians.[37]

At Greenville the Americans had drawn a definite boundary between themselves and the Indians, but there seems little reason to suppose that they intended this boundary to be permanent. The Indians were told that they could keep their lands as long as they desired, but it was a common belief in the American government that the pressure of white population would always make the Indians willing to sell. There was every indication that the promises made at Greenville and generally since 1789 had little real meaning. The ephemeral nature of the supposedly permanent Greenville line becomes particularly evident when one considers the position of the Connecticut Western Reserve and, to a lesser extent, the Virginia Military District. The western portions of the Connecticut Western Reserve, retained by Connecticut for her own use on ceding her land claims in the Northwest in September 1786, lay on the Indian side of the Greenville boundary line. It was exceedingly doubtful whether the United States had the right to divide land reserved by Connecticut, and it was quite obvious that further purchases would have to be made to satisfy Connecticut's promises to her own citizens.

Yet, in the Treaty of Greenville, no distinction was made between the land of the Western Reserve and the rest of the land relinquished to the Indians.[38] A similar situation existed in the northern tip of the Virginia Military District, which Virginia had reserved for her veterans in her cession to the United States Government in March 1784. The United States had assumed this obligation, but as in the case of the Western Reserve, no distinction was made between the tip of the Virginia Military District which was north of the Greenville line and the other lands yielded to the Indians.[39] The further cession, which in the case of the Western Reserve was obviously necessary, took place at Fort Industry in July 1805.[40] It was a purchase that had been inevitable ever since the Greenville Treaty had been signed.

The Treaty of Greenville, by bringing peace to the frontier and asserting the dominance of the United States in the Northwest, made possible the future American settlement of the area. In 1796 huge new Wayne County was carved out of the middle of the lands left to the Indians. As yet it was merely an administrative division, but it was quite obvious that it would in the future become much more.[41]

The rest of the decade was remarkably peaceful in the Old Northwest. The warlike Indians had once again to recoup their strength and confidence; others believed the promises made at Greenville and thought that this was indeed the last cession. Also, the British were no longer backing Indian resistance as they had done since the Revolution. By Jay's Treaty in November 1794 they agreed to withdraw from the northwest posts they had originally ceded in 1783, and as France and the United States flirted with war, Anglo-American relations became reasonably friendly.

But while the Indians were comparatively calm and boundaries relatively stable, American settlers poured across the Ohio into the land ceded by the Indians at Greenville. They were soon pushing up to and across the Greenville line, and all the promises of the early 1790's meant nothing. As had been prophesied, the Indians were to make further cessions, but they were made neither willingly nor peacefully.

The Ambivalence of
Thomas Jefferson

VII

THE POLICIES OF the 1790's had done nothing to assuage the basic problems of American-Indian relations. In the South there had been no relaxation of the pressure of settlement. The federal government had attempted to bring some order and justice into southern Indian relations, but its success was limited. Georgia had still not ceded her western land claims and resented all federal efforts to protect the Indians from overt extortion of land. This meant that any attempt to bring American civilization to the Creeks had to proceed under the constant threat of further pressure for land. Further to the north the Cherokees were in very much the same position. Tennessee settlers coveted the Cherokee land and were disinterested in any future well-being of the Cherokees; they had no desire to see the Indians own their own farms and achieve permanent ownership of lands that settlers had crossed the Appalachians to obtain.

In the North the Treaty of Greenville had provided a far more obvious turning point than any specific event in the South. In the 1780's the federal government had thrown its full weight into the effort to obtain lands northwest of the Ohio for sale and settlement. Greenville was the culmination of a twelve-year struggle. In the years following 1795 settlers streamed unhindered across and down the Ohio River. Though the Greenville line was supposedly inviolate, it was obvious by 1800 that some method would be found to secure further Indian cessions. In 1800 the Northwest Territory was divided—into the Ohio Territory, which was to become the present state of Ohio, and the Indiana Territory stretching far to the west.[1] Lands would soon be needed in the new Indiana Territory. Both in North and South the rush westwards went on unceasingly. One of the richest areas in the world awaited colonization, and the American frontiersmen, like all colonizers, were prepared to sweep aside whoever stood in their path.

President Adams had been fortunate in that the boundaries established in the two Washington administrations had opened land for American settlers and made it unnecessary for him to undertake extensive boundary revisions; the only exception to this was the 1798 Tellico Treaty with the Cherokees. But by the time Jefferson assumed the Presidency in 1801, the situation was rapidly changing. Settlers were overrunning land already obtained from the Indians and calling for new cessions. Jefferson soon discovered that as President he had to reconcile his ideals with the necessities of American interest.

To Jefferson the Indians were not inferior savages deserving to vanish before a superior people. "The proofs of genius given by the Indians of N. America," he had stated in June 1785, "place them on a level with Whites in the same uncultivated state." He had no hesitation in saying that he believed that the Indians were "in body and mind equal to the whiteman." In one sense Jefferson was prepared to go even further in his admiration of Indian society. "I am convinced," he wrote in 1787, "that those societies (as the Indians) which live without government enjoy in their general mass an infinitely greater degree of happiness than those who live under European governments." [2] Jefferson saw definite advantages in the supposed freedom of Indian life and felt it preferable to life under the monarchies and tyrannies of Europe. But Jefferson also saw American civilized life as being quite distinct from that of Europe. The United States had achieved both civilization and freedom, and the Indians, whom he believed to be the intrinsic equal of the white man, were now to be given the opportunity of progressing from their savage state to the far superior state of American civilization. Jefferson was time and time again to argue that if the Indians would give up their hunting society (he ignored the agrarian side of their culture) and accept the agricultural ways of the Americans, they could be absorbed, to their infinite advantage, within the American population.

Jefferson also envisaged that American expansion could be carried out with justice towards the Indian. "It may be taken for a certainty," he asserted in 1786, "that not a foot of land will ever be taken from the Indians without their own consent." But he did mention at the same time that though purchases would not be made every year they would be made "at distant intervals as our settlements are extended." [3] He did not explain what would happen if as the settlements extended the Indians decided to sell no land. Like Henry Knox, Jefferson tended to ignore unpalatable possibilities in his arguments; both were more than willing to envisage future expansion, but at the same time they insisted that all land cessions be obtained only with the clearest consent of the Indians. That these two might become incompatible was not allowed to influence the arguments. For both Knox and Jefferson the *deus ex machina* was the bringing of civilization to the Indians. Yet, on occasion, Jefferson was far more willing to speak bluntly and accept reality than Knox. "The two principles on which our conduct towards the Indians should be founded are justice and fear," he told Benjamin Hawkins in the summer of

1786, "after the injuries we have done them, they cannot love us, which leaves us no alternative but that of fear to keep them from attacking us. But justice is what we should never lose sight of, and in time it may recover their esteem." [4] Jefferson was able to support the military expeditions of the 1790's without any qualms and viewed them as an effective method of enforcing American policy.

As President, Jefferson discovered that he could not hope both to obtain the land he wanted and at the same time gain land only when the Indians were happy to offer it to the United States. The reasons for this were quite obvious. The first was the continual factor that American frontiersmen did not view Indians as potential farmers to whom the United States could offer the gift of civilization. To the frontiersmen Indians were savages who murdered, and tortured, and burnt. As the American population increased and more and more Americans decided to move to the West, the American government was inevitably faced with the decision of whether to turn the army against its own citizens or against the Indians. With Jefferson this perennial difficulty was compounded by his own vision and by the circumstances of his time. Jefferson had a great sense of American destiny; he saw a great nation stretching to the Mississippi and far beyond, a nation dedicated to freedom, a nation which would provide an example to the rest of the world. Moreover, he had a clear sense of the geopolitical realities of American expansion. By the time Jefferson became President the frontiersmen were pouring into the Ohio Valley, Kentucky and Tennessee. The rivers they were settling upon ultimately ran into the Mississippi, their outlet to the sea. The transfer of the Louisiana Territory from Spain to France in 1800 precipitated a crisis, but even without the transfer the demand for New Orleans, the navigation of the Mississippi and adjacent lands was obviously very near.

Jefferson had to fit the Indians into a scheme of American expansion and do it without violating his own concept of the mission of the United States to show Europe that a nation could live without war and could bring happiness to its people. That he viewed American expansion in terms of the spreading of civilization, the bringing of a new and better way of life, is not surprising.

Far more even than Knox he espoused the idea that the Indians were to be given the benefits of all that America had to offer. The sense of "Manifest Destiny," of moralistic expansion, is plainly evident in Jefferson's Indian policy. To Jefferson expansion was desirable not only for the Americans, but also for those whom it would engulf. This confidence often blinded Jefferson to the realities of everyday relations with the Indians. In speaking to a delegation of northwestern Indians in January 1809, at the very end of his Presidency when the Northwest was seething with discontent and Tecumseh was organizing his great confederacy to resist the demands of the American frontiersmen, he said: "I repeat that we will never do an unjust act towards you—On the contrary we wish you to live in peace, to increase in numbers, to learn to labor as we do and furnish food for your ever increasing numbers, when the game shall have left you. We wish to see you possessed of property and protecting it by regular laws. In time you will be as we are: you will become one people with us; your blood will mix with ours: and will spread with ours over this great island." [5]

In 1802 it was stated by Secretary of War Henry Dearborn that the three main reasons for sending agents to reside with the Indian tribes were to cultivate peace and harmony between the United States and the Indians, to defeat any illicit schemes by either Indians or whites, and to introduce husbandry and domestic manufacture "as means of producing and diffusing the blessings attached to a well regulated civil Society." [6] In his Second Inaugural Address in March 1805 Jefferson laid out quite clearly his views on the civilization of the American Indian: "The aboriginal inhabitants of these countries I have regarded with the commiseration their history inspires. Endowed with the faculties and the rights of men, breathing an ardent love of liberty and independence, and occupying a country which left them no desire but to be un-disturbed, the stream of overflowing population from other regions directed itself on these shores; without power to divert or habits to contend against it, they have been overwhelmed by the current or driven before it; now reduced within limits too narrow for the hunter's state, humanity enjoins us to teach them agriculture and the domestic arts; to encourage them to that industry which alone can enable them to maintain their place in existence and to prepare them in time for that state of society which to bodily comforts adds the improvement of the mind and morals." [7]

In pursuit of this object Jefferson frequently spoke at length to visiting Indian delegations on the delights of adopting the American form of civilization. He tried to provide the various tribes with agents to teach the men stock raising and crop cultivation and the women spinning and weaving. He never seemed to doubt that the Indians would be willing to accept the new way of life that was presented to them as preferable to the one they had, even though he himself had expressed the view that the Indians had many advantages in their uncivilized state and, in fact, were happier than civilized Europeans. In December 1808 he urged a delegation of Delawares, Mohicans, and Munsees to give up hunting: "Let me entreat you therefore on the lands now given you to begin to give every man a farm, let him enclose it, cultivate it, build a warm house on it, and when he dies let it belong to his wife and children after him." There was repeated emphasis on the concept of private property which would result in the establishment of an agricultural society for the Indians and lead to the intermingling of Indians and Americans. "You will unite yourselves with us, and we shall all be Americans," Jefferson told the Delawares. "You will mix with us by marriage. Your blood will run in our veins and will spread with us over this great island." [8]

Yet, though the bringing of civilization to the Indians was continually stressed in Jefferson's writings and speeches, the pursuit of land was there as well. The two became intertwined. Indeed, it was suggested that it might be best to obtain Indian land as extensively and as quickly as possible, for this would force the Indians to abandon hunting and live on smaller plots of land. By this means their advance to civilization would be accelerated. At times, in fact, Jefferson turned the whole emphasis around and suggested that the plan of civilization would be a good way to obtain land rather than stressing that the obtaining of land would promote civilization. In February 1803 Jefferson urged the agent to the Creeks, Benjamin Hawkins, to promote agriculture and household industry among the Indians, as hunting was already insufficient to furnish them with clothing and subsistence. "This will enable them to live on much smaller portions of land," argued Jefferson. "While they are learning to do better on less land, our increasing numbers will be calling for more land, and thus a coincidence of interests will be produced between those who have lands to spare, and want other necessaries, and those who have such necessaries to spare, and want lands. This commerce then, will be for the good of both, and those who are friends to both ought to encourage it." In this manner Jefferson could achieve American expansion and at the same time justify it as a positive good not only for the Americans, but also for the Indians. The Indians might not realize it, but it was the duty of the United States to educate them, to persuade them of the advantages of agriculture and domestic manufacture, and to accelerate their transition from a hunting to an agricultural economy by reducing the area of their land holdings. "I feel it consistent with pure morality," wrote Jefferson, "to lead them towards it, to familiarize them to the idea that it is for their interest to cede lands at times to the U.S., and for us thus to procure gratifications to our citizens, from time to time, by new acquisitions of land." [9]

Though it is clear that Jefferson would have liked to achieve success in bringing American civilization to the Indians and would have welcomed them as new American farmers, above all he desired land for American settlement and expansion. The United States was expanding across the conti-

nent, and Jefferson was willing to offer the Indians the benefits of the American civilization that was to supersede their
own way of life, but if they did not accept this offer, then they
would be swept aside. Jefferson desired that the Indians would
actually benefit from their loss of land, but at the last instant,
as might be expected, the land was more important than the
Indians.

Jefferson was very outspoken on this point in his message to
Congress on January 18, 1803. He stated that the Indian tribes
had for a considerable time been growing more and more
uneasy at the constant diminution of their lands, even though
this diminution of land had been effected by their own volun-
tary sales. As a result, the policy of refusing any further sales
had been developing among the Indians. In order "peaceably"
to counteract this policy "and to provide an extension of territory which the rapid increase of our numbers will call for,"
Jefferson suggested that two measures were expedient. The
first was to encourage the Indians to abandon hunting, adopt
stock-raising, agriculture, and domestic manufacture, and show
them that they could live better with less land and less labor.
This would persuade them that their extensive lands were
useless and that they should exchange them to obtain the
means for improving their farms and increasing their domestic
comforts. The second measure suggested by Jefferson was to
increase the number of trading houses and place within the
Indians' reach those things which would contribute more to
their domestic comfort than the possession of extensive but
uncultivated lands. By these measures the United States would
be preparing them ultimately to share in the benefits of the
American government. "I trust and believe," wrote Jefferson,
"we are acting for their greatest good." [10]

At the time of this message Jefferson was of course under
particular pressures in American foreign relations. The news
that Spain had ceded the Louisiana Territory to France had
been a profound shock, so much so that the President had
talked of a possible alliance with England.[11] Jefferson considered it essential that as France would soon be in control of

the Mississippi the United States should reach that river with all possible speed and counteract potential French influence among the Indians. In February 1803 he told Governor William Henry Harrison of the Indiana Territory that the cession of Louisiana to France would make the Indians reluctant to make further land cessions. "Whatever can now be obtained," wrote Jefferson, "must be obtained quickly." He repeated his arguments for the encouragement of agriculture and domestic manufacture among the Indians and then was particularly blunt in his description of the benefits of extending trading houses. He said he would be glad to see influential Indians run into debt at these trading houses, for when the debts were more than they could pay, they would be willing to settle them by a cession of land. Jefferson added that he would like to see the purchase of all the land along the Mississippi.[12]

What is perhaps surprising is not that Jefferson attempted to combine the bringing of civilization and the acquisition of land, but that he took such an optimistic view of the success of this attempt. Though there was some success among the Cherokees and Creeks, for the most part the policy to bring civilization was a dismal failure. The effort and money expended were never very great, and it asked the impossible in expecting the Indians to suddenly throw off their way of life and happily accept another as superior or even moderately desirable. Yet, Jefferson persisted in speaking as though the whole policy was a striking success. "Our Indian neighbors are advancing, many of them with spirit, and others beginning to engage in the pursuit of agriculture and household manufacture," he wrote in his annual message of December 1805. "They are becoming sensible that the earth yields subsistence with less labor and more certainty than the forest, and find it their interest from time to time to dispose of parts of their surplus and waste lands for the means of improving those they occupy and of subsisting their families while they are preparing their farms." [13]

This simply was not true. By the end of 1805 the northwestern Indians were ready to listen to the arguments of

Tecumseh and the southern Indians were trying to dig in their heels to resist the continual request for cessions of land. Yet, Jefferson continued to talk as though the Indians were acquiescing readily or even joining happily in the cession of land and the abandonment of their hunting grounds. In December 1806 he announced, "We continue to receive proofs of the growing attachment of our Indian neighbors," and in November 1808 that "the attachment of the Indian tribes is gaining strength daily." [14] In fact, in December 1808, near the end of his Presidency, after the Indians had been pressured into ceding large areas of land beyond the Greenville line, Jefferson told a chief of the Delawares that the United States still looked with reverence upon the Treaty of Greenville: "I assure you, that the U.S. will for ever religiously observe the treaty on their part, not only because they have agreed to it, but because they esteem you." [15]

The only time that Jefferson had seriously suggested a variation of his policy was in the summer of 1803 after he had received news from Paris that the United States had bought the vast Louisiana Territory. Then Jefferson suggested that Indian lands east of the Mississippi be exchanged for lands west of the Mississippi north of the thirty-first parallel. In this way American expansion east of the Mississippi could continue unimpeded and the chance of white-Indian friction would be eliminated. In fact, Jefferson went so far as to suggest that the Indians be given a constitutional guarantee of their right of soil west of the Mississippi. This was never done, as Jefferson's cabinet objected both to a constitutional amendment in regard to the Louisiana Purchase and to giving the Indians constitutional rights in the land. Jefferson on several occasions wrote of the idea of Indian removal in the summer of 1803, but his interest did not last. Though it was revived on a number of occasions in his discussion with the southern tribes, Jefferson, for the most part, abandoned removal and returned to his original plan of civilization as a means of obtaining the land east of the Mississippi.[16]

The acquisition of the Louisiana Territory did, however,

present Jefferson with the task of dealing with a whole new series of Indian tribes. In his contacts with these Indians of the trans-Mississippi West Jefferson was less enthusiastic in wanting to bring civilization. When in July 1804 Peter Chouteau was appointed as Indian agent for the District of Upper Louisiana, Secretary of War Henry Dearborn told him to encourage all the Indians to accept the idea of agriculture and domestic manufactures. But in Jefferson's speeches to chiefs of the trans-Mississippi West who visited Washington he did not emphasize the advantages of civilization, though this formed the main burden of his addresses to the delegations from east of the Mississippi. Jefferson told a group representing the Osage it would be of advantage to both the United States and the Indians to engage in commerce and useful intercourse. He also requested them to be friendly to American explorers who were going to be sent into the land west of the Mississippi. In fact, in discussions with the nations west of the Mississippi Jefferson consistently talked of the advantages of trade and peace and only occasionally introduced the matter of adopting the way of life of the Americans.[17] In other words, the pressure and persuasion for adoption of American civilization were exerted far more strongly on those Indians whose lands were wanted more immediately by the American government. Time was of the essence, for the Indians had to be acculturated before they were swept aside by the American frontiersmen. Jefferson, like Knox, continued to hope against most visible evidence that this might be accomplished. He never admitted, and probably never realized, that he was asking for the impossible.

The South, 1799—1809

VIII

EVEN THOUGH they had already ceded more than they wished, the Indians of the South experienced increased pressure in the late 1790's. Tennessee's admission to the Union in 1796 stimulated settlement in that area, and the creation of the territory of Mississippi in 1798 gave full warning to the Indians that the American nation intended to continue expanding westward. Moreover, the government soon became intent on establishing firmer communications with the distant territory of Mississippi, and this necessitated still more pressure on the Indian tribes. In May 1799 the Secretary of State, Timothy Pickering, informed the governor of the territory, Winthrop Sargent, that he had been urging the Postmaster General to take action on the establishment of a mail service between Natchez and Nashville (there was already a regular mail service as far as Nashville). As this would entail a route through—and several way stations in—the Indian country, the Secretary of State asked Governor Sargent to ascertain its feasibility.[1] The government was anxious to link its possessions southwards from Tennessee to the Gulf, but it was not until after Thomas Jefferson assumed the Presidency that any real action was taken.

The general superintendency of southern Indian affairs had been given to Benjamin Hawkins in 1796. This appeared to be a most reasonable appointment as Hawkins had frequently expressed sympathy for the Indian predicament and an understanding of their point of view. "I can assure you there is nothing I have more at heart than the preservation of them [the Indians]," he had written to Jefferson in June 1786, "it is a melancholy reflection that the rulers of America in rendering an account to Heaven of the aborigines thereof will have lost every thing but the name." [2] Hawkins did make a genuine attempt to bring civilization to the Indians. But in spite of his feelings the lands of the southern tribes were to suffer a sharp reduction in size during the time he served them. In the years immediately prior to Jefferson's presidency, Hawkins, like Governor Sargent, was to determine whether or not the southern Indians would agree to further concessions. The Secretary of War, Samuel Dexter, asked him in December 1800 to find out if the Creeks would be willing to sell the land south of the Altamaha and the land between the Oconee and Ocmulgee rivers. If Hawkins thought it would be indiscreet to ask, he was to report why.[3]

Immediately after Jefferson assumed power his Secretary of War, Henry Dearborn, emphasized that the new government intended to combine expansion with the bringing of civilization. On May 15 he told Return J. Meigs, who was being appointed Indian agent to the Cherokee nation, that "It has been a principal object of the Government of the United States to introduce among their Indian Allies useful arts, to teach them industry and prove to them its value experimentally by facilitating the attainment of articles considered to be of comfort and convenience in civilized life." [4] Yet, in little over a month, three commissioners—James Wilkinson, William R. Davie, and Benjamin Hawkins—were appointed to negotiate with the Chickasaws, Choctaws, and Cherokees.

Congress had in February 1799 and May 1800 provided money for new Indian treaties, and Jefferson now used this in an attempt to obtain land and roads which were particularly desired by Tennessee and Georgia. The message that Henry Dearborn sent to these Indians did not mention land cessions, it merely asked them to send men in whom they had confidence and who had the power to agree to such proposals of the commissioners as they might think proper.[5] The instructions that were sent to the commissioners on June 24, 1801, were far more specific.

The first object of the negotiation with the Cherokees was to gain Indian lands for the state of Tennessee—in particular the land in northern Tennessee separating the settlements in the east of the state from those south of the Cumberland and also land to the west of the Cumberland settlement, between the Cumberland and the Tennessee rivers. Moreover, the commissioners were to obtain Cherokee permission for a road from the boundary towards Natchez through the Cherokee country to the edge of the Choctaw country, along with permission to establish two or three white families on the road. If the commissioners could not gain agreement on any of the original demands for land, then they were to try to persuade the Cherokees to cede all their land north of a road from Knoxville to the Nashville settlements. If even this was unacceptable, then the commissioners were instructed to try to obtain a strip of land one to five miles wide for the running of this road across their lands. Use of such a road had been granted to the United States by the Treaty of Holston. If nothing else, then the commissioners should press for the establishment of three to four families on the Knoxville-Nashville settlement road. If either the first three proposals or the alternatives could be obtained, the commissioners were authorized to pay the Cherokees five thousand dollars immediately and one thousand dollars annually in goods (in addition to their present annuity).[6]

A week after these instructions had been issued to the commissioners a Cherokee delegation visiting Washington expressed distrust of future American intentions. This delegation told the Secretary of War that they were happy after boundaries had been drawn following the Treaty of Tellico, but that now they understood another treaty had been authorized to deprive them of more land: "We think that the United States do not want our lands; but we know well who do want them—the frontier people want them." How can we raise stock as we have been encouraged to, asked one Cherokee chief, if we part with more land? The Secretary of War tried to placate the Cherokee delegation. He said that though the white people were very numerous and wished to buy land when the Indians wanted to sell, the government considered all land beyond the present Indian boundary line "as absolutely belonging to our Red Brethren." He assured them that they would not be forced into anything that was disagreeable to them. He did say, however, that when lands that the Indians would not sell separated American settlements, then the United States wanted roads and way stations through Indian territory. Dearborn also encouraged them to abandon hunting in favor of agriculture and stock-raising and tried to ease their fears regarding the effects of the new roads.[7]

On July 3 Dearborn wrote to the commissioners and said that the second object of the instructions, the alteration of the boundary line from the Ohio between the Cumberland and the Tennessee rivers, should be postponed. He also urged the commissioners to introduce the subject of roads and settlers on them with great care and persuade the Indians that the United States did not wish to purchase lands unless the Indians wanted to sell. They were even to say that the United States was not in want of lands, but only desired roads. It is not surprising that when the Cherokee deputation left Washington on July 10, Dearborn wrote to their agent Return J. Meigs to say that frequent Indian visits to the seat of government should be checked, for it was frequently the source of vast expense without resulting good.[8]

The instructions of June 24 regarding the Chickasaws and the Choctaws did not receive such prompt protests. The commissioners were told that the object of their mission to the Chickasaws was to secure consent for the proposed road to Natchez and for the establishment of two or more white families upon it. As yet, there was to be no pressure for the cession of land by the Chickasaws, though as in the case of the Cherokees the government could expect that the establishment of a road, and the resulting white-Indian contact, would facilitate future land purchases. This philosophy had long been expressed, and there was no doubt that the establishment of a network of communications on the Indian side of a boundary line was an aid to future demands for cessions.

The commissioners were ordered to be particularly careful with the Choctaws. Dearborn referred to them as one of the most powerful Indian nations within the limits of the United States. "A pacific and friendly disposition in and towards them should be cultivated," he wrote, "as well from principles of policy as of humanity." The commissioners were to stress that the Choctaws had received two thousand dollars last year and that a similar appropriation had been made for this year, even though they had no claim to this money by any treaty. It could then be pointed out, Dearborn suggested, that as they had given nothing for this money, and as it might be taken away, it would be proper for the Choctaws to grant something to the United States. In essence, the commissioners were to try to obtain Choctaw permission for a road through their country to Natchez, permission for three or four families to settle on the road to accommodate travellers and post riders, and Choctaw recognition of the cession in the Natchez area east of the Mississippi and north of the thirty-first parallel which originally had been made to the British in 1765.

In general, the commissioners were to place great stress on the obtaining of the proposed Nashville-Natchez road, which would be used for both mail and travellers. The road would cut right through Cherokee, Chickasaw, and Choctaw country. Otherwise, the main emphasis was on any land cessions that could be obtained from the Cherokee to allow for the expansion of the state of Tennessee. Dearborn realized well the suspicion with which the southern Indians were regarding any demands for land, and he was willing to accept merely the road without land cessions, if pressure for land would arouse the southern tribes.[9]

On July 17, 1801, Dearborn sent the commissioners their instructions for negotiating with the Creeks. Here land was of primary importance, for the state of Georgia was, as usual, eager to take every possible inch. The principal object of the negotiations was to obtain the cession of land south of the Altamaha River. Dearborn called this cession of great importance and said the commissioners could pay twelve thousand dollars in goods as well as a two thousand dollar increase in the Creek annuity. The commissioners were also to discover on what terms the Creeks might cede the land in the Ocmulgee Fork and ask Dearborn for further instructions. Another difficulty had been created by the Treaty of New York in August 1790. At that time it had been agreed that the true source of the main, south branch of the Oconee River would be discovered, and though this had been accomplished (with some disagreement), some settlers were on the land that had been declared Indian by this decision. The commissioners were to try to get the line adjusted to include the settlers on the Indian side of the boundary line.[10]

The negotiations proved even more difficult than had been expected. The Cherokees, from whom most was wanted, yielded nothing. On September 5, 1801, Doublehead told the commissioners that the Cherokees did not want roads through their country because a great many people would pass along them and cause trouble. The commissioners, who had been warned by Dearborn that they should proceed with great caution, retired unsuccessfully from the Cherokee conference.[11]

The conference with the Chickasaws took place in the middle of October at Chickasaw Bluffs, Tennessee. On this occasion the commissioners were able to obtain permission for the Nashville-Natchez road (though they could not get agreement for way stations), and were even able to compensate for their lack of success with the Cherokees by confirming the definition of Chickasaw lands which had been made by President Washington on July 1, 1794. Under this definition, the Nashville-Tennessee River part of the road, which the United States had attempted to obtain permission for from the Cherokee, fell within Chickasaw territory. The commissioners reported that the Chickasaw nation was of an "amicable and orderly disposition," but that they had not advanced so far in civilization as their neighbors, the Cherokees. They said, however, that the Chickasaws were progressing in this regard, and they supported Chickasaw requests for a number of articles to aid civilization. "We, with great deference, submit these claims of the Chickasaws to the consideration of Government," wrote the commissioners, "and, were it not presumptuous, we would earnestly recommend to the councils of our country, a steady perseverance in that humane and beneficent system, which has for its object the civilization, and consequent salvation, of a devoted race of human beings. The prospects of success become daily more flattering, but, to ensure it, an extension of the means, and a reform in the application, may become necessary." [12]

The Choctaws also proved reasonably amenable to the demands of the American commissioners. In the middle of December 1801 at Fort Adams, in Mississippi Territory, they agreed to the road through their lands, though as in negotiations with the Chickasaw, the commissioners did not overcome Indian resistance to the settlement of white families along the road. But the Choctaws did agree that the old cession to the British on the lower Mississippi would form the boundary between them and Mississippi Territory. The commissioners reported that both Choctaws and Creeks were worried by new settlements along the western banks of the Mobile and Tombigbee and thought it necessary that the government should define the extent of the cessions already made by the Indians on the Mobile, Tombigbee, and Alabama rivers. They also reported that the Choctaws were discovering that the destruction of game was making their hunting extremely precarious and that for the first time they had requested tools and implements. "These circumstances induce us to cherish the hope," wrote the commissioners, "that, by the liberal and well directed attention of Government, these people may be made happy and useful; and that the United States may be saved the pain and expense of expelling or destroying them." In spite of all the assertions that the Indians had absolute right to their lands and could keep them or sell them as they wished, the commissioners had no doubt that the Indian lands would be acquired either by civilization of the Choctaws or by their expulsion or destruction.[13]

The first treaties of the Jefferson Administration had been moderate ones, and the commissioners had proceeded gently when faced with signs of Indian resistance. Yet, pressure was being exerted, and as the need became greater, it obviously would be increased. Greater pressure was already needed in Georgia, where state impatience for Creek land had increased in proportion to federal caution. The Creeks resisted whenever possible, and as they could not be assembled for the proposed treaty in late 1801, the conference was delayed until the following year. In the spring of 1802 Dearborn asked the commissioners to postpone their negotiations (this time until late in May) in order to give Georgia time to send an agent to the treaty meeting and to furnish such financial aid as the state might want to give. "It is deemed important to satisfy the Government and citizens of Georgia," wrote Dearborn, "of the real sincere disposition of the General Government to make every exertion in its power for obtaining the cession of the several tracts of land as contemplated by the proposed Treaty." The commissioners were to make every effort to impress this upon the minds of the agents and citizens of the state.[14]

Dearborn at the same time sent the commissioners more instructions for their negotiations with the Creeks. As in the previous year he stated that the first object of the negotiation was the obtaining of the land south of the Altamaha River. Dearborn, with strange confidence, stated that he expected that the Creeks would not want large compensation as Georgia had already bought the tract from them. He now said that he expected ten thousand dollars at the treaty and a fifteen hundred dollar annuity would probably be enough. Secondly, the commissioners again were to press for the tract of land between the Oconee and the Ocmulgee rivers. In fact, if necessary, the commissioners could yield the western part of the land south of the Altamaha if they felt that by this they could obtain the Ocmulgee Fork. For this cession, the commissioners could pay twenty-five thousand dollars at the treaty and an annuity of two thousand dollars. Thirdly, the commissioners were to press for an adjustment of the northern boundary line in order to include settlers who were on the Indian side of the boundary; this was particularly designed to include those settlers around the Currahee Mountain. For this land the commissioners could pay three to five thousand dollars and an annuity of three to five hundred dollars. The Creeks were again to be subjected to considerable pressure.[15]

On April 24, 1802, Georgia at last officially ceded her western land claims to the United States Government. As part of the settlement the federal government agreed to extinguish, "as early as the same can be peaceably obtained on reasonable terms," the Indian title to land south of the Altamaha, lands left out when the United States-Creek line was drawn in 1798, and the lands between the forks of the Oconee and Ocmulgee rivers. It was stated in the act of cession that a meeting was to be held immediately with the Creeks for this purpose. Moreover, and here the United States doomed the Creeks, it was stated that the United States "shall, in the same manner, also extinguish the indian Title to all the other Lands within the State of Georgia."[16]

The Creek treaty did not proceed as smoothly as Dearborn had hoped. The first problem was that the land around the Currahee Mountain belonged to the Cherokees, not the Creeks. This meant that the third object of the proposed treaty could not be achieved. The commissioners did, however, attempt to carry out the remainder of their instructions, and the treaty was finally signed at Fort Wilkinson, Georgia, on

June 16, 1802. Though the Creeks were exceedingly reluctant to cede land, they finally agreed to a part of the demands of the United States Commissioners. Many of the Lower Creeks did not attend the treaty and this was used as an excuse by those who did attend for not yielding all of Tallassee County. They said they could not yield the land below Rock Landing and south of the Altamaha, and the commissioners told Dearborn that they agreed because of the arguments of the Indians and because Georgia placed a greater value on the land above Rock Landing. The commissioners also had to settle for less than half of the land between the Oconee and the Ocmulgee rivers.[17]

Though the Creeks resisted the full demands of the American commissioners, the lands they retained were still under considerable pressure. The commissioners reported that the Creeks wanted American soldiers posted on Indian lands to hold back American settlers and commented that not only would this prevent incidents between whites and Indians, but it would also familiarize the Indians with the idea of land cessions. The commissioners were hopeful that the Indians were beginning to accept the idea of American agricultural civilization.[18]

The Choctaws, who in 1801 had defined their western boundary on the lower Mississippi, agreed to a demarcation of their eastern boundary at the Convention of Fort Confederation in October 1802. Once again the Americans used as the basis of the settlement a Choctaw cession to the British nearly forty years before. It was agreed that the Choctaw cession in 1765 of land between the Tombigbee and Chickasawhay rivers would now be plainly retraced and remarked. This remarking was carried out within a year, and in August 1803 at Hoe Buckintoopa the details of the line were recognized by James Wilkinson and Choctaw commissioners.[19]

The year 1802 had produced only moderate cessions, but the news of the transfer of the Louisiana Territory from Spain to France persuaded Jefferson that acquisition of Indian lands should proceed with all possible speed both north and south of the Ohio. Former qualms of angering the Indians became less important as the President looked towards the Mississippi and in 1803 both Creeks and Cherokees were subjected to severe pressure. On February 19 Dearborn told Agent Return J. Meigs that the opening of a road between Georgia and Tennessee had become "highly necessary." The road was to run from the headwaters of the Oconee to South West Point, or a spot between there and the Tellico blockhouse. There were also to be way stations along the road. Dearborn said that the permission for this from the Cherokees should not cost more than five hundred dollars, perhaps with additional presents, "but at all events we must have a road." Dearborn gave Meigs remarkably naive arguments to use with the Cherokees. He first told Meigs that the Cherokees should be as friendly as the Chickasaws and Choctaws, who had given permission for a road through their territory, and he pointed out that all nations in time of peace were willing to have their neighbors pass through their countries. "We shall not consider the Cherokees as good neighbours," wrote Dearborn, "unless they will allow their best friends who are taking every means in their power to make them happy, to make a road at their own expense to pass through their Country from one settlement to another." Friendship notwithstanding, the Cherokees quickly turned down this request in the spring of 1803. They made it quite clear in these early years of Jefferson's Administration that they did not want roads through their territory.[20]

At this point the idea that the Cherokees had the full right to agree or disagree with suggestions of the federal government collapsed. Dearborn wrote to Meigs on May 30 and told him that the Cherokees would have to be "brought to reason" on this subject by the bribery of one or two influential chiefs. Dearborn suggested that if some of the chiefs were induced to support the American proposal then it should be easy to obtain general consent. To achieve this end, Dearborn suggested it might be proper "to offer an inducement" to Vann and one or two other chiefs. It was no surprise when in the fall of 1803 the Cherokees agreed to the Georgia-Tennessee road.

The futility of Indian resistance was never more effectively demonstrated.[21]

The comparative caution that had been demonstrated towards the southern Indians in 1801 and 1802 evaporated in the years from 1803 to 1806. The pressure was such that it made a farce of the oft-repeated assertion that the Indians were equally free to sell or refuse to sell. The Cherokees quickly discovered that the road to which they had agreed was only a beginning. In April 1804 Dearborn appointed Meigs and Daniel Smith to be joint commissioners for holding a treaty conference with the Cherokees. They were given orders to attempt the acquisition of such land within the states of Tennessee, Kentucky, or Georgia as could be obtained on reasonable terms; they were particularly to seek the land separating the settlements of eastern and western Tennessee, and the land near Currahee Mountain.[22]

These renewed efforts to obtain land from the Cherokees were justified by Dearborn on the grounds that it would be greatly to their advantage. "It is believed," he wrote, "that the money & goods which they will receive for the lands more especially that part which will be paid annually, will be of more real benefit to the Nation under their improved state than the lands can be." Dearborn took the position that as the Cherokees had advanced more than other tribes in adopting American civilization, the United States could best serve them by removing their lands as rapidly as possible. "They will be enabled to make still a greater progress in the useful arts," he wrote, "and will more & more rely on Agriculture and domestic manufactories for their support and of course become a happier people." Once again, as in the question of a road through Cherokee territory, Dearborn suggested a little judicious bribery: "I am induced to believe that Vann has very great private influence on the nation," he wrote. "I am therefore very desirous that some measures may be taken to interest him in favor of our views." Dearborn elaborated on this idea in a letter to J. W. Hooker, factor at Tellico. He authorized him to use two or three hundred dollars, if by any particular civilities to Vann he could induce him to favor cessions of the Cherokee lands between East and West Tennessee and in the region of Currahee Mountain.[23]

The result of all this was obvious, and in the following years the Cherokees, though showing great reluctance, were obliged to relinquish more of their territory. The Treaty at Tellico in October 1804 was not a success for the federal government, for though the United States did at last obtain the land around Currahee Mountain, the Cherokees did not relinquish the land separating the eastern and western settlements of Tennessee.[24] Another attempt to obtain the land was made in the early summer of 1805 and failed, for the price offered the Indians for land had not been raised. On the eve of the renewal of negotiations in the fall, Dearborn told Meigs to remember that the highest price the United States would pay for the cession of Indian claims "well situated & of good quality, is two cents per acre," and that lesser lands ought not to bear a higher price in proportion to their value.[25]

The negotiations in the fall of 1805, with the United States again making sure that influential chiefs were rewarded, proved more lucrative. In two treaties signed at Tellico on October 25 and 27 the Cherokees finally ceded the large area separating East Tennessee settlements from those on the Cumberland and the rest of the land between the Cumberland and Duck rivers. (Some of this area had been ceded earlier in the year by the Chickasaws.) The Cherokees also agreed to two more roads: one to run from Stone River to meet the Georgia road toward the southern frontier of the Cherokees, the other to run from the neighborhood of Franklin via Muscle Shoals to settlements on the Tombigbee.[26]

Cherokee lands were diminishing rapidly, and those left were steadily being criss-crossed with American lines of communication. When a delegation of Cherokee chiefs visited Washington in January 1806 Jefferson took the opportunity to praise them for their adoption of American ways. The Cherokees, of course, had had no choice. Those who wanted to save themselves had to adopt the idea of private property, agriculture, and stock raising. (Of course, in the long run, even this was not to save them.) Moreover, aside from the elicited praise, the Washington meeting produced a very large cession of land between the Tennessee and the Duck rivers. Once again this was an area claimed by both Cherokees and Chicka-saws, the latter having the most substantial claim.[27]

The Secretary of War communicated to Agent Meigs on January 8, 1806, one day after the Cherokee cession, that the President was giving one thousand dollars to Chief Double-head of the Cherokees "in consideration of his active influence in forwarding the views of Government, in the introduction of the arts of civilization among the Cherokee Nation [of] In-dians, and for his friendly disposition towards the United States, and for the purpose of enabling him to extend his useful example among the Red people." [28] Though this was to be the last Cherokee cession before the War of 1812, there was no doubt that their control of lands in the Tennessee country had been effectively broken during Jefferson's presidency. The Cherokees had been more successful than other Indian tribes in adopting the ways of American civilization, and their suc-cess was used as another argument for removing their remain-ing lands. For a time it seemed that many would survive owing to their adoption of private property, but this too was eventually to collapse under the pressure for land.

While the resistance of the Cherokees was being under-mined, the Creeks also were feeling the usual pressure. The cessions they had made at Fort Wilkinson in the summer of 1802 were viewed as totally inadequate by Georgia, and in February 1803 Dearborn told Hawkins that he should do ev-erything in his power to persuade the Creeks to cede the rest of the land between the forks of the Oconee and the Ocmul-gee. The United States, pointed out Dearborn, was under an obligation to take all fair and prudent means in its power to secure from the Creeks an extension of the present Georgia boundary between those two rivers. As was Dearborn's prac-tice, he presented his agent with ready-made arguments for use with the Creeks. Hawkins should tell the Creeks that "a mere mathematical line in the woods" could never prevent cattle of both sides from straying where they pleased; a strong natural boundary (the Ocmulgee) would serve the Creeks far better. Also, wrote Dearborn, "the Creeks should recollect that our Government is at a very great expense annually on their account, and they ought to show a friendly disposition towards us." Dearborn could see "no good reason" why the Creeks should refuse the obvious advantages of a natural boundary such as the Ocmulgee.[29]

In May 1803 three commissioners were appointed to negoti- ate with the Creeks. They were to obtain as much of the land between the Oconee and the Ocmulgee as possible, but they were to devote particular attention to obtaining the tract be- tween the western boundary obtained at Fort Wilkinson and the Ocmulgee. This would give the United States a natural boundary, a convenient site for a military post and trading factory, and the advantage of transport on a navigable river. Later in May Dearborn wrote to Hawkins praising the progress in the introduction of civilized arts among the Creeks. He thought it proved the practicality of so improving the state of society among the Indians that all distinctions between "what are called Savages and civilized people" could be de- stroyed. But Dearborn also wrote of more immediate concerns. He was worried by reports that the Creeks, Cherokees, Chicka- saws, and Choctaws were considering holding their lands in common. Hawkins was to make every effort to resist such a combination; Dearborn thought it would be much better to reverse the process and have the Indians divide their lands among their principal towns, with each town having com- plete control over its own lands. Then further subdivision could provide individual families with enough land for cultivation.[30]

For all the talk of the advantages of a natural boundary, the Creeks balked at suggestions of further cessions between the Oconee and Ocmulgee. They refused to yield any more land, and in the fall of 1803 it was necessary to make arrangements to run the boundary settled at Fort Wilkinson in the previous year.[31]

But the issue was of course not yet closed, and in the spring of 1804 Hawkins was again given the task of obtaining more of the Oconee-Ocmulgee land and, if possible, land in Tallassee County. To ensure that Hawkins did his best, General David Merriwether was sent to represent Georgia at the council. During the winter of 1803-1804 Hawkins had already been given the task of obtaining Creek agreement for a road to run through their country connecting Washington with New Orleans. But the Creeks again put up a determined resistance to American pressure, and Hawkins was unable to obtain a satisfactory treaty. Though he did finally obtain a small cession, he paid more than was customary for the Indian land, and the treaty was not ratified by the Senate.[32]

In 1805 the matter rose again. In February Dearborn informed Hawkins that the Senate had refused to ratify his treaty, and he now tried a different approach. He told Hawkins that as it was highly important that the lands between the Oconee and the Ocmulgee be obtained from the Creeks, and as some chiefs had shown an interest in coming to Washington, Hawkins should bring them to the capital during the summer. "The Chiefs should come," wrote the Secretary of War, "with authority, not only to make a cession of the land in question, but to consent to the opening of a road through their Country." [33] The Creeks had now on numerous occasions exercised the right, which the federal government had frequently and explicitly given to them, of saying "no" in matters of the land cessions. They had already shown far more tenacity than most tribes, but now they were to be brought to Washington, hopefully to be overawed by the power of the United States.

In November 1805 the Creek chiefs appeared before the President in Washington. Jefferson told them that since the Treaty of New York in 1790 the United States had endeavored to promote their well-being, especially by encouraging them to adopt agriculture and domestic manufacture. "You will certainly find your interest," he went on to say, "in selling from time to time, portions of your waste & useless lands, to enable you to procure stocks and utensils for your farms, to improve them, and in the meantime to maintain your families. . . . We are a growing people, therefore whenever you wish to sell lands, we shall be ready to buy; but only in compliance with your own free will." After saying that everything depended on the free will of the Creeks, he returned to the old question of the lands between the forks of the Oconee and Ocmulgee rivers. He said the United States both at Fort Wilkinson in 1802 and in Hawkins' negotiations had attempted to obtain a strong natural boundary—the Ocmulgee. The Indians had agreed to sell land in Hawkins' negotiation, but Jefferson pointed out that the price was so outrageous that the Senate had declined to ratify the treaty. The Creek delegation had been asked to come to Washington, Jefferson said, to discuss this matter and see if "a reasonable price" could be agreed on. After announcing that the United States still sought the Oconee-Ocmulgee lands, Jefferson then gave his arguments for a road from Washington to New Orleans through Creek lands, saying that among whites it was usual for people of one nation to have free and innocent passage through another.[34]

The Creek reply to Jefferson was given one day later by Chief McIntosh. He described the Oconee-Ocmulgee area desired by the United States as "a large tract of land & valuable land." He also neatly countered Jefferson's arguments regarding price. The American government, argued McIntosh, was perhaps paying too much attention to what had been done by the forefathers of the Creeks: "We find since we have grown up," he said, "they partly gave their land away,—we now find they have gave so much of it away, we have but little left to set down on—We now begin to know the value of land—But when it is almost too late." McIntosh was, of course, on exceedingly strong ground, as the United States had been refusing to pay the Indians more than two cents an acre for even the best land, though the government charged its own western settlers two dollars an acre. "We the chiefs here present," spoke McIntosh, "consider that if you, the White people, had such land to dispose of, and the Red people had to buy it of you, you, we are convinced, would not let us have it, without you got the full value for it." McIntosh's arguments were far more convincing than those of Jefferson and he continued by describing the actual process of gradual expansion theoretically stated by Washington and Knox in the 1780's. After the Treaty of New York, McIntosh asserted, when the Oconee was made the boundary, even though Washington placed troops at Fort Wilkinson to keep out settlers, they quickly had their cow pens, their hogs, and their hunters on the Indian side of the boundary. Even before the Creeks sold the land at Fort Wilkinson in 1802, argued McIntosh, the grass and corn was nearly all destroyed for ten or fifteen miles back from Fort Wilkinson up to the high shoals of the Apalachee. The Ocmulgee will perhaps be the same, argued McIntosh, as this natural boundary would prove as ephemeral as a marked line. McIntosh also opposed the road through Creek country.[35]

Though even the Creek chiefs who came to Washington had expressed opposition to United States demands, and though Jefferson had said that the Creeks could act of their own free will, two weeks of federal negotiation were enough to bring about major changes of mind if not of heart. On November 14 the Creeks ceded the desired land between the Oconee and Ocmulgee to the United States and also agreed to a horse path through the Creek country from the Ocmulgee to the Mobile.[36] Thus, after several years of sustained pressure the United States had obtained the land it desired. Though Creek signatures had been obtained on the treaty of cession, it could hardly be said that they had ceded the land of their own "free will." The Creeks, like the Cherokees, had been subjected to continuous pressure, and it was not surprising that both these tribes submitted to this pressure and judicious bribery.

With the continuous advance of American settlers and increased American interest in the Mississippi River, the Choctaws and Chickasaws also found themselves subject to forceful persuasion in the years from 1802. Jefferson submitted to the Senate in January 1803 the Fort Confederation Treaty of October 1802 which involved the land between the Tombigbee and the Chickasawhay rivers. He also reported to the Senate that the government was engaged in ascertaining the former Choctaw cessions from the Yazoo River to the southern United States boundary and that he expected a new cession of lands "of considerable extent" between the Tombigbee and Alabama rivers.[37]

In February 1803 Dearborn wrote to James Wilkinson suggesting the desirability of further Choctaw cessions. It seemed likely that the Choctaws would be willing to cede lands as a means of paying their very heavy debts to the trading house of Panton, Leslie & Co. Though the Choctaws were in fact willing to cede lands in order to pay their debts, they were not interested in ceding the particular lands which the United States wanted along the Mississippi.[38]

The Choctaws and the Chickasaws had benefited by their distance from the main advance of American settlement, but in 1803 their comparatively favorable situation was quickly altered by the Louisiana Purchase. These tribes which had long known that behind them was the reasonably friendly power of Spain now found that Americans had the opportunity to develop large settlements in the West. This obviously meant not only pressure for lands, but also pressure for roads to establish communications with settlements on the Mississippi. Jefferson went out of his way to win Choctaw friendship when a delegation visited Washington in December 1803, for he said that "It is hereby announced and declared, by the authority of the United States, that all lands belonging to you, lying within the Territory of the United States shall be and remain the property of your Nation forever, unless you shall voluntarily relinquish or dispose of the same." While the Choctaw delegation was in Washington it expressed willingness to cede lands as a means of paying its large debt to Panton, Leslie & Co., and Jefferson answered that the United States would like all the lands she could obtain along the Mississippi and would appoint agents to negotiate for a cession. In the meantime he asked the Choctaws to follow the American example in agriculture which would be far more beneficial to them than hunting.[39]

As American settlers had not yet reached Choctaw lands, the government was, for the time being, only interested in a cession of land along the Mississippi and showed an unusual lack of interest in other Choctaw cessions during 1803. It was argued in 1804, however, that the Mississippi Territory was too isolated from the rest of the United States and that there were other reasons for additional cessions. It was pointed out that settlers on the west bank of the Tombigbee River had for many years been permitted to raise crops on the east bank, but that the Fort Confederation Convention in October 1802 had confirmed the east bank of the Tombigbee to the Choctaws. It was suggested that the government should extinguish Indian title to a tract on the east bank of the Tombigbee River and that the Indians should listen to reasonable terms, as the tract included no Indian settlements and most of the game had been driven off.[40]

Finally, in the fall of 1804, Dearborn informed agent Silas Dinsmoor that commissioners would be appointed to hold a treaty conference with the Choctaws. One can almost see Albert Gallatin hovering in the background as the instructions for estimating a fair price for Indian lands were given. Dearborn suggested ascertaining the annual profit the Indians obtained from hunting a certain tract and probable profits for the next fifty years. If the Indians had an annual profit of three thousand dollars then they could be given an annuity of three thousand dollars a year or a sum which would bring them that amount in interest per year. "It may however be very fair and proper," wrote Dearborn, "to make very considerable deductions from the present hunting profits on account of the constant decrease of the game, especially as the annuities will never be diminished and as the labor and trouble of procuring peltries and fur by hunting will be saved." [41]

It was not until the spring of 1805 that Commissioners James Robertson and Silas Dinsmoor were sent instructions for negotiating with the Choctaws and Chickasaws. The Secretary of War told them that the object of the proposed treaties was highly interesting, not only to the United States, but also to Tennessee and the Mississippi Territory. He enclosed a petition from the principal chiefs of the Choctaws asking the United States to purchase as much of their land between the mouth of the Yazoo and the Chickasaw nation as would satisfy their debt to Panton, Leslie, & Co. The United States was interested in the part between the Mississippi and the Big Black Rivers, and Dearborn suggested that it might amount to three and a half or four million acres, for which a two thousand dollar annuity was suggested as the highest that should be paid, in addition to both the debt and the treaty expenses.

The commissioners were next told that the object of the proposed treaty with the Chickasaws was to obtain all land claimed by that tribe north of the Tennessee River, or as much of it as the Chickasaws would cede. Also, if practicable, the commissioners should obtain all Chickasaw lands north of a line from the mouth of the Duck River due west to the Mississippi. If this cession could not be obtained, the commissioners should ask for, in addition to the lands north of the Tennessee River, the Chickasaw lands north of the south line of Kentucky, between the Tennessee, Mississippi, and Ohio Rivers. Dearborn thought the Chickasaw lands north of the Tennessee would probably amount to some three and a half to four and a half million acres (though much of this land was also claimed by the Cherokees). As a rule of thumb he suggested that if the Chickasaws should prove to have four million acres north of the Tennessee, of which three-quarters was undisputed, the commissioners could pay them not more than twelve thousand dollars to pay their debts, ten thousand dollars in goods for their own use, and a two thousand dollar annuity. Dearborn also suggested ways for ensuring some Chickasaw support for these cessions: The commissioners could make a separate article with the king of the nation to pay him one hundred dollars annually for life, also they could pay two thousand dollars to Chief George Colbert for his relinquishing the privilege of keeping ferries over the Tennessee and Duck rivers and give him an additional annuity of sixty dollars. Dearborn added that it might not be improper to let these chiefs know of the plans early in the negotiations. If Colbert had objections, then the commissioners were to persuade "the King" and other chiefs to assert a right to the ferries. Dearborn advised extremely moderate prices, in keeping with his other suggestions, for the other cessions that he hoped would be made by the Chickasaws.[42]

These high hopes for treaties with the Choctaws and the Chickasaws proved a severe disappointment. Though the Choctaws had wanted to pay their debts to Panton, Leslie & Co., they did not want to cede lands in which the United States was interested and refused to do so at a conference in June. The Secretary of War was angered by the complete failure of these expensive negotiations, and he blamed Silas Dinsmoor, agent to the Choctaws, for purchases that far exceeded what had been contemplated. Dearborn spoke of the "extraordinary articles"—raisins, anchovies, cinnamon, nutmegs, pickles—that had been bought for an Indian treaty "in the woods"; however, he said that as the Choctaws had requested the treaty and the Upper Choctaws had ruined the chances of a settlement, the entire treaty expense should be charged to the Upper Choctaws. The Lower Choctaws, who had been willing to sign an agreement with the United States, were, on the other hand, to be told that they would not be charged. However, the Secretary of War quickly took steps to place the Choctaws under new pressure, for he asked Dinsmoor to discover from Chief Homastubbee what the Lower Choctaws would cede, and for what amount, and suggested that special consideration be given to Homastubbee himself: "It may not be improper to make liberal propositions to Homastubbee, separate from the general stipulations; as he is entitled to attention." [43]

The Chickasaw treaty was somewhat more successful than the Choctaw one, for though the Chickasaws would not cede all the land that the United States wanted, they did cede tracts north of the Tennessee in a Chickasaw Bluffs treaty of

July 23, 1805. Once again writing to James Robertson on July 3, 1805, the Secretary of War advocated bribery as a means of breaking down Indian resistance: "if any particular individual among the Chickasaws, who may be opposed to the proposed Cession of lands, and who may have considerable influence with the nation, can be induced to change the direction of his influence, by any reasonable means, the Commissioners will please to act in such cases, as circumstances may require." In the treaty that was signed on July 23, one thousand dollars was given to Chiefs Colbert and Ockoy and a one hundred dollar annuity to Tinebe.[44]

In the late fall of 1805 the commissioners again attempted to obtain land from the Choctaws. It was hoped that even if they would not cede the land along the Mississippi, at least it might be possible to obtain land along the lower Tombigbee. But even now the United States could not obtain the particular lands it desired, though on November 16 at Pooshapukanuk the Choctaws made a large cession of lands in what is now southeastern Mississippi and southwestern Alabama. As this was not the area for which the commissioners had been instructed to negotiate, Jefferson would not submit the treaty to the Senate until January 1808, but then it was ratified.[45]

Though treaties had been signed with the Chickasaws and the Cherokees in July and October 1805, the Secretary of War had to write to James Robertson on May 15, 1806, and tell him that no appropriations had yet been made to carry them into effect. Dearborn confidently expected that such appropriations would be made in the next session of Congress, but in the meantime he adjudged that the Cherokees and the Chickasaws would probably feel uneasy, especially when settlements were made on the land ceded in these treaties. It was not until March 1807 that the Secretary of War was able to inform the agent to the Chickasaws, Thomas Wright, that appropriations had at last been made for carrying into effect the treaty signed in July 1805.[46]

From 1801 to 1806 Jefferson had obtained a vast area of land east of the Mississippi from the four main southern tribes. The treaty with the Cherokees in January 1806 was to be the last formal land cession made by those tribes before the War of 1812. Yet, American pressure continued and the process of gaining sure control over all the land east of the Mississippi was carried forward. In September 1806 the Secretary of War found a new method of dealing with Indian resistance to the establishment of way stations on roads they had reluctantly granted through their country. Dearborn told Benjamin Hawkins that in the establishment of a mail line through the Creek country to New Orleans it was necessary to have stations where horses and riders could be refreshed. As the Creeks had shown resistance to any such proposal, Hawkins was told that the contractor for mail on the route would secure proper persons for establishing these stations and that Hawkins should give them trader licenses for the Indian country. "As those licensed persons will go into the Country in the character of traders," wrote Dearborn, "I presume there will be no other considerable difficulty in fixing the stations than the particular location of them." Hawkins was further instructed that if presents to some of the principal chiefs would be necessary or useful, he was authorized to spend up to six or seven hundred dollars.[47]

Dearborn used the same notion of a few judiciously distributed presents when in 1807 he arranged for the boundary lines that had been established by the treaties with the Chickasaws and Cherokees to be run. He had discovered that whereas the whole waters of the Elk River had been included in the Chickasaw cession, this river was east of the Cherokee cession. He stated, therefore, that the line should not be insisted upon without Cherokee consent but that it would be very desirable if the Cherokees would cede it for a moderate payment. Dearborn then made it very clear that this need not be the willing act of the whole Cherokee nation when he said that this extra cession should be obtained "provided they will consent to it for some handsome presents to the Chiefs who may accompany you on the line." Only two or three chiefs were to accompany the surveying party, and Dearborn stipulated that one of them should be Doublehead, who had already received payment from the United States for his part in previous cessions.[48]

Great effort was made to keep the friendship of those chiefs who had proved amenable to the idea of cession and who were willing to accept ill-disguised bribes. Dearborn also specified that in running the Chickasaw line, Chief George Colbert should accompany the surveying party, and he arranged for Colbert's son to be placed in a school in Washington for three or four months.[49] Such efforts to secure the allegiance of influential chiefs were methods of ensuring that when treaties were desired, there would always be American advocates within the Indian ranks. These efforts usually brought the desired results and in the running of the Cherokee line in 1807 it was agreed that the Elk River area would be included, though it had not been ceded at the original treaty. For this the Cherokees received an additional two thousand dollars, and one thousand dollars and two rifles went to the chiefs who had agreed to the additional cession.[50] The frequently expressed idea that the United States would never obtain Indian land without their consent, that it was theirs to sell or refuse to sell, lost all meaning when accompanied by such tactics as these.

In the remaining years of Jefferson's presidency settlers moved into those areas that had been ceded in the 1801-1806 period and began the usual process of encroaching beyond the boundary lines on to the land that had been left to the Indians. The Cherokees, who lay across the path of the rapidly expanding state of Tennessee, were subject to particular pressure and for them Jefferson even revived the idea that Indians could be removed beyond the Mississippi River, a practice he had first introduced after the Louisiana Purchase. The Secretary of War suggested in a letter to Cherokee Agent Meigs on March 25, 1808, that he should embrace every opportunity for sounding out the Cherokee chiefs on the subject of whether they would exchange their present land for a tract on the other side of the Mississippi. Jefferson again discussed this possibility when the Cherokees visited Washington in May

1808. He also talked to chiefs of the Upper Cherokees about their proposal that their lands be formally separated from those of the Lower Cherokees and that they become citizens of the United States. Furthermore, he said that if it became possible, the minority who did not want to take the step toward American civilization could move west of the Mississippi; however, Jefferson seemed distinctly hopeful in the last years of his administration that many of the Cherokees would be willing to throw off their old ways and become frontier farmers.[51]

In a similar way, high hopes were expressed for the civilization of the Creeks. The Secretary of War wrote to Benjamin Hawkins in May 1808 that he was pleased with the progress of civilization among that tribe: "A few years more of persevering attention will no doubt demonstrate, the error of those opinions which have so generally prevailed in our Country, on the subject of the civilization of the Aborigines—Generations yet unborn will have abundant reason for blessing the memory, of your character, for having contributed so essentially, to the amelioration of their Condition." But it was never forgotten that Hawkins was also trying to smooth the path for expansion. In December he was asked to secure Creek approval of another mail route—this time from East Tennessee to the Tombigbee. "It is presumed," wrote Dearborn, "that moderate presents to some of the most influential Characters, will be deemed sufficient for so trifling a favor." To Dearborn such methods of obtaining Indian agreement had become the rule rather than the exception—showing clearly the extent to which the consent of whole "Indian nations" was being obtained in formal treaties.[52]

For all the hopes of civilization and peace, the ominous news from the Indian country in the last years of Jefferson's presidency was that, in spite of the huge cessions that had been made since the turn of the century, the encroachment of white settlers onto Indian lands was once again angering the southern tribes. Though the government ordered its agents to procure the removal of such settlers, they continued to come.

More than a few military forts and an occasional military expedition were needed to stop them. In March 1809 at the conclusion of Jefferson's presidency, the news from Tennessee was that settlers on Chickasaw lands were increasing daily and that the Indians were complaining of frequent intrusions.[53] Land and more land was desired by the southern settlers, and at the last instant the government found itself obliged to fulfill their desires, whatever the wishes of the Indians.

The Old Northwest,
1795—1809

IX

THE TREATY OF GREENVILLE brought only temporary respite from Indian problems in the Old Northwest. It was obvious that those settlers who were crossing the Ohio River in large numbers would not be content to leave unoccupied the desirable lands that had been left to the Indians in 1795. This became particularly apparent in 1800 when the Northwest Territory was divided into Ohio and Indiana territories. Indiana Territory, whose first governor was William Henry Harrison, stretched over a vast area which was still nearly all in Indian hands. Harrison soon made it obvious that he had no intention of leaving it that way.

At least on paper the Jefferson Administration made no distinction between the objects of its policy northwest and southwest of the Ohio. When William Lyman was appointed an agent in the Old Northwest in July 1801 Dearborn told him that it was a principal object of the government to introduce useful arts among the Indians and he spoke of the extent to which this was succeeding south of the Ohio. "We trust to prepare them for the enjoyment of a higher degree of happiness," he wrote, "than any of which they could be susceptible of if left to themselves." To achieve this it was necessary to introduce spinning and weaving among the women and farming and stock raising among the men.[1] Though the program of civilization northwest of the Ohio never achieved even the limited success it had south of that river, Jefferson proceeded after 1801 as though this was a practicable policy and could form the basis of Indian relations in the Old Northwest.

It was soon apparent after 1800 that the great pressure that had been exerted on the northwestern Indians from 1783 to 1795 was to be renewed. The beginning of negotiations for land beyond the Greenville line partially resulted from an Indian request, a request which they hoped would safeguard the rights they had been granted in that treaty. In the winter of 1801-1802 Chief Little Turtle of the Miamis, along with chiefs of other northwestern tribes, visited Washington and conferred with the Secretary of War. On January 4 Little Turtle spoke on behalf of the visiting delegation and expressed concern about the boundaries of the land owned by the United States around Vincennes in Indiana Territory, for in the Greenville Treaty it had been agreed that the Vincennes tract, though beyond the Greenville line, would be granted to the United States to the extent that it had previously been held by the French and the British. Little Turtle, however, expressed the fear that some whites were settling beyond the bounds of the tract and asked that a firm boundary line be drawn. Furthermore, he requested ploughs and various tools and said that if these were granted the chiefs would introduce husbandry. On January 7 Jefferson told the visiting delegation that the United States would take great pleasure in furnishing implements and instructors so that the Indians could learn to cultivate the earth, raise animals, spin, and weave. "These resources are certain," said Jefferson, "they will never disappoint you, while those of hunting may fail, and expose your women and children to the miseries of hunger and cold." [2]

Dearborn quickly reacted to Little Turtle's request and to the new interest in expansion beyond the Greenville line. On January 23, 1802, he wrote to Harrison to say that the various tracts obtained at Greenville, particularly the Vincennes tract, should be defined and that Harrison was to ascertain the boundaries. In doing this he was told to consult the Indian chiefs and to make sure that they were satisfied that no more land was enclosed than was justified by the treaty.[3]

However, before Harrison could proceed in regard to the Vincennes tract, he received other instructions from the Secretary of War about tracts on the Indian side of the Greenville line. On June 17, 1802, Dearborn informed Harrison that the President wanted him to act as an agent for the United States in designating the boundaries of the two tracts at or near Fort Wayne ceded to the United States at Greenville. He was to try to put the two tracts—one at Fort Wayne of six miles square and the other of two miles square embracing the navigable waters of the Maumee and the Wabash—in the most advantageous positions possible. Harrison was to consult Little Turtle and other chiefs on the manner of fixing these boundaries. On this same date Dearborn also gave Harrison more detailed instructions as to what should be asked for in negotiating the boundaries of the Vincennes tract.[4]

Harrison wasted no time in attempting to obtain generous boundaries for the Vincennes tract. In the fall of 1802 he obtained a preliminary agreement by which the Indians, under protest, granted an extensive cession around Vincennes, and he gained Indian assent to American possession of the salt spring on Saline Creek below the mouth of the Wabash on the Ohio. However, in these preliminary negotiations Harrison set the course which was to cause bitter American-Indian relations in the Old Northwest in the next decade. Harrison was a powerful negotiator and, once given the authority, rode roughshod over Indian resistance. Dearborn told him in February 1803 that a deputation of Delawares and Miamis who had visited Washington during the winter had complained loudly of the unfair means used for obtaining the assent of some of the chiefs to the proposed boundaries.[5]

Up to this point the Jefferson Administration had demonstrated moderation in dealing with Indians in the Old Northwest. All the instructions to Harrison had urged that he treat the Indians fairly and obtain only what had been given to the United States in the Treaty of Greenville. Though there were already signs that Harrison's method of negotiation was capable of producing angry protest, the central government had not as yet expressed any official desire to shatter the agreement that had been made at Greenville. In the winter of 1802-1803 this picture changed as a direct result of the transfer of the Louisiana Territory from Spain to France. The news of this secret cession gave Jefferson a vital interest in the acquisition of land bordering the Mississippi River and made him far more direct in the matter of Indian land acquisition. The first clear sign of this was in Dearborn's letter to Harrison of February 1, 1803, when he told Harrison to take the earliest opportunity for conferring with the nation or nations claiming the lands in the vicinity of the Kaskaskias and a tract bordering on the Mississippi and the Ohio, and to try and obtain a cession of these lands. Dearborn added that he had heard that French and Spanish agents had been among the Indians last autumn to try to persuade them to be hostile to the United States.[6] Six days later Jefferson himself wrote to Harrison making it quite clear that an emergency situation had been created by the transfer of the Louisiana Territory from Spain to France and that the land would have to be obtained before French influence was brought to bear on the Indians. He plainly told Harrison that he quickly wanted all the land along the Mississippi and suggested that influential Indians be encouraged to run up debts at the trading houses so that they could later pay them in land.[7]

Having received this letter from the President, Harrison could well believe that he now had the power to use all possible methods to obtain Indian land cessions, and in the summer of 1803 he carried out treaties for which he had been given full authority. The first of these was signed at Fort Wayne on June 7, 1803, and it confirmed the preliminary agreement arranged in the previous fall. The list of signatory tribes was imposing: the Delaware, Shawnee, Potawatomi, Miami, Eel River, Wea, Kickapoo, Piankishaw, and Kaskaskia. These tribes agreed to cede a large tract of land around Vincennes (far more than the Indians thought they were ceding at Greenville), the salt spring on Saline Creek below the mouth of the Wabash on the Ohio, three tracts for way stations on the main road between Vincennes and Kaskaskia, and one tract for a way station on the road between Vincennes and Clarksville. In August the cessions for way stations were concurred in by the Wyandots and reconfirmed by the Eel Rivers, Piankishaws, Kaskaskias and Kickapoos.[8]

The Kaskaskias, who had long been reduced to a pitiful remnant, ceded all their extensive holdings in the Illinois country, except for two fairly small tracts, on August 13. This large cession of land in what is now southwestern Illinois, stretched from the Ohio up to and well beyond the Kaskaskia River. Jefferson reported the cession in his Third Annual Message of October 17, 1803, commenting that "The friendly tribe of Kaskaskia Indians, with which we have never had a difference, reduced by the wars and wants of a savage life to a few individuals unable to defend themselves against the neighboring tribes, has transferred its country to the United States, reserving only for its members what is sufficient to maintain them in an agricultural way." The Kaskaskias were, in fact, a decimated and impotent tribe; indeed there was considerable doubt as to their rightful claim to all the land they had ceded.[9]

Once the Greenville line had been broken, cessions proceeded regularly. By 1809 Harrison obtained much of what is now southern Indiana and a considerable part of present-day Illinois by what were nominally cessions granted by the Indians of their own free will. In June 1804 Dearborn told Harrison that he was empowered to negotiate with other Indian nations whose claims might interfere with the boundaries of the Kaskaskia cession. "You will take such measures," wrote Dearborn, "and make such pecuniary advances to individual Chiefs or others as their respective cases require." Having suggested the customary sweetener, Dearborn demonstrated quite clearly that whatever the public assertions of Jefferson and his government, the Greenville line was becoming meaningless. Dearborn suggested that "it may not be improper" to obtain from the Sacs such cessions on both sides of the Illinois River as might entitle them to an annual compensation of some five or six hundred dollars. For this, Dearborn suggested that the Sacs should relinquish all claims to any land on the southern side of the Illinois and a considerable tract to the north.

This was only the beginning. Dearborn also urged Harrison to encourage the principal chiefs of other nations to follow the example of the chief of the Kaskaskias and to pay particular attention to the Piankishaws, for their lands divided the Vincennes tract on the Wabash from the cessions of the Kaskaskias on the Mississippi. Moreover, it would also be desirable, suggested Dearborn, to obtain the tract between the southern line of the Vincennes territory and the Ohio River. Harrison was to embrace every opportunity to obtain any portions of these suggested additions to American territory. Dearborn also sent for Harrison's consideration a suggestion of the President that it might be more expedient to give annuities to each Indian family rather than annuities to the entire nation, even if this meant giving an aggregate of fifteen or twenty percent more. There was of course ample reason for this suggestion: Jefferson was doing all he could to encourage an Indian adoption of private property rather than tribal ownership of land, and the measure was not the financial sacrifice that it appeared at first glance. It was once again a cautious step which befitted an administration whose Secretary of the Treasury was Albert Gallatin. In fact, Dearborn pointed out to Harrison that when a family became extinct the annuity would cease, and when the members of a family decreased its annuity would decrease proportionately. As observers had frequently pointed out that

Indian tribes were decimated in the presence of the advancing frontiersmen, there seemed little danger of any financial catastrophe.[10]

With this mandate from the Secretary of War, Harrison soon obtained more land. On August 18, 1804, at Vincennes, the Delawares ceded what is now the southwestern corner of the state of Indiana—between the Vincennes tract, the Wabash, and the Ohio. Nine days later, on August 27, the Piankishaws agreed to cede this same tract to the United States, and at the same time they acknowledged the right of the Kaskaskias to sell the country ceded at Vincennes on August 13, 1803.[11]

In the Old Northwest the United States had far more trouble than in the Southwest with the problem of conflicting Indian land claims. There was some difficulty in the South, particularly in regard to land claimed by both Cherokees and Chickasaws, but it was in the Northwest that the government had most to concern itself with the extinction of several different claims to the same area. This problem arose from the number of tribes in the Old Northwest (increased by those who had been pushed westwards by the advance of the frontier), their mobility, and a natural desire on their part to make the federal government pay for as much land as possible. Harrison attempted to clarify this situation and in the Vincennes Treaty with the Delawares even stated formally the extent of Delaware lands, but it was to prove extremely difficult to persuade the other tribes to agree to any statement of land ownership made by Harrison on behalf of the United States Government.

Harrison did not stop in 1804 with the land south of the Vincennes tract; he also followed another of Dearborn's suggestions and dealt with the Sacs and Fox. For this negotiation Harrison proceeded to St. Louis and had excellent success in obtaining what Dearborn had suggested. The Sacs and Fox in November 1804 ceded not only their claims to the land south of the Illinois River, but also a great stretch of land north to the Wisconsin River. This meant that claims to what is now northwestern Illinois and even to what is now southwestern Wisconsin had been yielded.[12]

Since 1803 Harrison had made tremendous strides towards obtaining the land to the Mississippi that Jefferson had asked for in February of that year. From the Kaskaskias and the Sacs and Fox he had obtained land stretching along the Mississippi from the Ohio to the Wisconsin River, and the Piankishaws had acknowledged the right of the Kaskaskias to cede the land of what is now southwestern Illinois. Rather than the tribes of Indiana looking eastward to the solid barrier of the Greenville line, they now had to look over their shoulders to the Mississippi, for the United States had bypassed them, and it was quite obviously only a matter of time until they themselves would be obliged to succumb to American pressure.

While Harrison was following the instructions of Jefferson and Dearborn, by relentlessly pressing the tribes of the Northwest for the cession of more lands, Jefferson himself retained a roseate view of the proceedings, at least in his public messages. In his Annual Message of November 8, 1804, he explained the Delaware cession of land between the Vincennes tract and the Ohio: "That tribe, desiring to extinguish in their people the spirit of hunting and to convert superfluous lands into the means of improving what they retain, have ceded to us all the country between the Wabash and the Ohio." This was an exceedingly optimistic view of the proceedings. Moreover, still other Indian tribes looked askance at the cessions made by the Delawares and the Piankishaws. Little Turtle and his Miamis considered that they too had a claim to the land south of the Vincennes tract, and they made their feelings known in the fall of 1804.[13]

The process of obtaining the lands guaranteed to the Indians by the Treaty of Greenville proceeded rapidly in 1805. Once again the Indians nominally ceded the lands of their own free will, but the rapid transference of land aroused bitter opposition. On April 2, 1805, the Secretary of War appointed Charles Jouett as commissioner to hold treaty negotiations with the Wyandots, Ottawas, Chippewas, and any other

Indians who might have a claim to the lands bordering on the southwest part of Lake Erie between the Cuyahoga and the Maumee and southward to the Greenville line. The principal object was to satisfy not the state of Ohio, but the Connecticut Land Company. This company wanted the chance to buy the Indian title to land west of the Cuyahoga which Connecticut had retained as part of her Western Reserve when she ceded her western land claims to the federal government. This Reserve was the area between the Cuyahoga and a line one hundred and twenty miles west of the western boundary of Pennsylvania and between the forty-first and forty-second degrees of north latitude. Jouett was ordered to see that everything was fair and just and to use his influence to induce the Indians to make a cession on reasonable terms of the lands claimed by the Connecticut Company. Dearborn, as in the South, was little inclined to placate the Indians by over-generous payments for their lands. He pointed out to Jouett that the price usually given for the Indian lands did not exceed one cent an acre and that, except for some particularly desirable tracts, the government was in no case inclined to give more than two cents an acre. If the agents of the company wanted to give the Indians more, Jouett was not to prevent it, but it would be better, urged Dearborn, if they were to pay from one to two cents an acre. If the Indians would also yield land between the Connecticut Company claims and the Greenville line, Jouett was authorized to negotiate for it at not more than two cents an acre. He was also authorized to negotiate for land between the Sandusky and the Maumee.[14]

In the winter of 1804-1805 there had been definite signs that the Indians of the Northwest had been displeased by the cessions of 1803 and 1804, but little was done to pacify those who were anxious. In June Harrison was informed that the government intended to locate and survey the various tracts ceded to the United States ten years before at the Treaty of Greenville, and he was to notify the chiefs so they could attend the survey.[15] All was astir beyond the Greenville line; lands had been ceded, further cessions were being planned, and now the surveyors were to move in to mark out the variety of cessions made at Greenville. It was quite obvious that the Greenville line had served its purpose (settlers had moved rapidly onto the American side of it without Indian hostility) and now the next step forward was to be taken.

The negotiations undertaken for the Connecticut Land Company proved a success. At Fort Industry on the Maumee on July 4, 1805, the Wyandots, Ottawas, Chippewas, Munsees, Delawares, Shawnees, and Potawatomis ceded the remaining land of the Western Reserve; everything north of the Greenville line between the Cuyahoga and a line one hundred and twenty miles due west of the western boundary of Pennsylvania.[16] In the following month Harrison signed what was becoming his annual treaty with the Indians, this time at his home, Grouseland, near Vincennes. By the Treaty of Grouseland, which was signed on August 21, 1805, the Miamis, Eel Rivers, and Weas ceded to the United States a large tract in what is now southeastern Indiana. This linked the land obtained at Greenville with the Vincennes tract and with the land south of the Vincennes tract ceded by the Delawares and Piankishaws in August 1804. Moreover, the Potawatomis, Miamis, Eel Rivers, and Weas acknowledged the right of the Delawares to cede the land south of the Vincennes tract by the treaty of August 18, 1804. The Miamis, however, did not allow the definition of the remaining Delaware lands which had been given by Harrison in that treaty to stand. They stated that they had only intended to make the Delawares tenants at will of the land between the Ohio and White rivers, not invest them with the right of soil. Accordingly, the Delawares released the United States from the guarantee of Delaware lands that had been given in the treaty one year before.[17]

The Secretary of War was delighted that any doubts about the Delaware-Piankishaw cession of the previous year had been removed and that the United States now owned all the land bordering the Ohio River above the mouth of the Wabash. He urged Harrison to continue with his efforts to obtain land and told him that he was directed by the President to secure from the Piankishaws as soon as possible their claim to the land between the Wabash and the eastern boundary of the Kaskaskia cession. Harrison had proposed this shortly after signing the Treaty of Grouseland. Given this order, Harrison proceeded rapidly. On December 30, 1805, at Vincennes, the Piankishaw ceded their claims to the land in what is now southeastern Illinois between the Vincennes tract and the cession made by the Kaskaskias in August 1803.[18]

While the land of the Old Northwest fell with increasing rapidity within the grasp of the United States, Jefferson continued to urge the Indians of the region to adopt civilization. In January 1806 he told the chiefs of the Sacs, Fox, and Potawatomis who were visiting Washington that they should follow the example of their southern brethren and take up agriculture and abandon wars. The government also encouraged the Indians of Indiana to take up farming and supported agents who were given the task of teaching agriculture and stock raising to Indians who were often bitterly opposed. When in April 1806 Nicholas Boilvin was appointed as sub-agent to the nations of Indians residing on the Mississippi above the mouth of the Missouri, he was told to try to teach them agriculture and the arts of domestic manufacture. There was already a government agent among the Sacs aiding them in adopting farming techniques.[19]

The Secretary of War continued to instruct Harrison to negotiate for more land and the President still talked of the Indians gradually adopting the ways of civilization, but the truth of the matter was that the Indians of the Old Northwest were becoming increasingly dissatisfied with the wholesale attempts to advance the American frontier from the Greenville line to the Mississippi. In 1805 the Shawnee Prophet began to preach resistance to the ways of the Americans at Greenville, and very soon his brother Tecumseh was to transform a religious revival into an attempt at Indian unity against the Americans. Infuriated by the piecemeal cessions obtained by William Henry Harrison, Tecumseh was to make the cornerstone of his movement the idea that the Indians held their land in common and that cessions by individual tribes were invalid. This movement of the Prophet and his brother began to gain ground after 1805, but this stiffening resistance did not alter the basic objects of American policy. The Secretary of War appeared chagrined by the whole affair. "It is excessively mortifying," wrote Dearborn in July 1806, "that our good faith should so frequently be called in question by the natives who have it in their power to make such proud comparisons in relation to good faith." [20]

Mortifying or not, three days later Dearborn was issuing instructions to William Hull, Governor of Michigan Territory, for a new treaty with the Indians. Hull was ordered to negotiate for two tracts. The first was the whole of southeastern Michigan, an area which Dearborn thought would amount to from four to five million acres; the other was in northwestern Ohio, from the western boundary of the Connecticut Western Reserve to the Maumee. This second proposed cession, Dearborn suggested, would amount to some eight or nine hundred thousand acres of which some two hundred thousand acres were to be reserved to the Indians for farming. Dearborn asked Hull to try to calculate the price so that in no case would it exceed two cents an acre, and hopefully the price would be one cent an acre. The first area was looked upon as the primary object of the negotiation; if the chiefs of the Wyandots and Ottawas did not want to cede the area in northwest Ohio, then that object of the negotiation should be given up. [21]

The problems of negotiating with the Indians were well-illustrated by the fate of these instructions to Hull. After waiting four months for an acknowledgement, Dearborn reached the conclusion that the instructions might have miscarried, and six months later, on January 27, 1807, he was obliged to renew them. This second set of instructions met with a better fate than the first, and finally, on November 17, 1807, Hull was able to obtain the first object of his mission by a treaty with the Ottawas, Chippewas, Wyandots, and Potawatomis at Detroit. These tribes agreed to cede a large tract of land stretching northward from the Maumee, in northwest Ohio, across southeastern Michigan.[22]

By 1807 not only had most of Ohio been ceded to the United States, but also large tracts of southern Indiana, Illinois, and Michigan. One cession had even stretched northward into what later became Wisconsin. Much of this land had been obtained by intense American pressure. From early 1803 Jefferson had determined to push firmly and rapidly towards the Mississippi, and he had given his agents full power to seek lands from the Indians of the Old Northwest. Though Harrison was a hard negotiator (and has justly gained a reputation as an enthusiastic garnerer of all possible land), there is no doubt that he received ample support in his policies from the federal government.

In spite of this Jefferson wrote his public statements as though the Treaty of Greenville was still sacrosanct and that the United States was only obtaining land which the Indians were delighted to give. He said to the Shawnees in February 1807 that since Greenville "some of them [the Indians] have thought it for their advantage, to sell us portions of their lands which has changed the boundaries in some parts; but their rights in the residue remain as they were and must always be settled among themselves." He then proceeded to lecture on the advantages of agriculture and domestic manufacture and was pleased that the Shawnees had expressed a determination to assume the American way of life.[23] In spite of these optimistic statements, the plan of civilization had gained little ground in the Northwest by the summer of 1807. Rather than the northwestern Indians happily and readily accepting the plans for American civilization, the religious revival of the Shawnee Prophet was now gaining ground with a program of throwing off the ideas and ways of the whites and returning to "primitivism." Though Harrison blamed all this on the activities of British agents, and though the British agents were from the fall of 1807 to take advantage of this situation, the basic cause of the growth of Indian resistance was of course the program of aggrandisement which had brought about the breakdown of the Greenville boundary line.[24]

The process of winning control of the land beyond the Greenville line went on in spite of Indian resistance, and it went on with expressions of confidence that the Indians were quite happy with the condition of affairs. On November 25, 1808, at Brownstown, the Chippewas ceded a tract of land one hundred and twenty feet in width from the foot of the rapids of the Maumee to the western line of the Western Reserve for a road and all the land within one mile of the road on each side to allow the establishment of settlements. No more effective way could have been devised to ensure American penetration of the entire area served by the road. These tribes also ceded to the United States a tract of land for a road (but this time without the land for settlements) to run south from Lower Sandusky to the Greenville line.[25] In contrast to the area south of the Ohio, where the four main tribes strongly resisted roads and settlements beyond the boundary line, the Old Northwest was interlaced with tracts for forts and a network of communications. Both in the North and South the running of roads, mail routes, and trading posts behind the official line was an effective way of preparing for further cessions. The Indians of the Old Northwest had bitterly opposed American demands from 1783 to 1794, and by 1807 they were again preparing to fight for their lands. But for all this, in the last years of his presidency Jefferson still hoped for the success of his civilization policy and even spoke as though it was, in fact, winning success in the Old Northwest.

On April 22, 1808, Jefferson wrote to the chiefs of the Ottawas, Chippewas, Potawatomis, Wyandots, and Senecas of Sandusky to explain the views of the government. He said that ill blood had remained between the Americans and the Indians after the Revolution and not until the Treaty of Greenville was a solid peace and perfect understanding attained. Since then, said Jefferson, they had looked upon the Indians as brothers. The United States had tried to persuade the Indians to cultivate the earth and spin and weave because she had seen that game was becoming too scarce to support them: "to encourage you therefore to save yourselves has been our constant object." Nevertheless, pointed out Jefferson, the Indians had been free to do as they pleased with their lands; they could sell or refuse to sell, and this right of choice would never be violated by the United States: "When a want of land in a particular place induces us to ask you to sell, still, you are always free to say 'No,' and it will never disturb our friendship for you." [26]

Jefferson spoke in a similar vein to Little Turtle, the Miami Chief, who visited Washington in December 1808. Jefferson said he had always considered it an act of friendship to buy Indians' lands when they wanted to sell, whether the Americans wanted the land or not, because the purchase price enabled the Indians to improve the land they retained. In the same month he told Beaver, Chief of the Delawares, that the United States would always observe the Treaty of Greenville.[27] But while Jefferson spoke of agriculture and friendship in December of 1808, his plans for civilization in the Old Northwest seemed further than ever from completion. On December 22 Dearborn fired William Kirk because the object of his appointment among the Indians had not been realized and no prospect existed of its early attainment. Kirk had been employed to show the Indians in the region of Fort Wayne how best to farm and adopt other ways of white civilization. But the effort continued, and five days later the Secretary of War appointed Captain Hendrick, a Stockbridge Chief, to assist the Delawares in domestic arts.[28]

When Jefferson left office in March 1809, he could look back on tremendous gains in land both south and north of the Ohio. Though large tracts of land were still held by the Indians, it was quite obviously just a matter of time before American settlers would pour over the whole eastern half of the Mississippi Valley. This had already been prepared for by large land acquisitions along the Mississippi itself. Jefferson's attempt to combine his vigorous land policy with a program of civilization for the Indians had met with far less success. In the North its impact was so slight as to have little real effect. In the South it was more successful, particularly among the Cherokees, and to some extent among the Creeks, but even here, most Indians bitterly resented the constant pressure on their lands and saw American policy as one of land acquisition rather than the bringing of civilization. Both in the North and South there were signs of stiffening Indian resistance, and by the end of Jefferson's presidency Tecumseh was making rapid strides toward building an Indian confederacy in the North and was prepared to extend it into the South.

In spite of all this Jefferson exuded confidence. He never hinted that American policy could have anything but the best interests of the Indians at heart. He argued strongly that the taking of lands speeded the process of Indian civilization and therefore was desirable. Apart from the difficulty of resolving the true motives in this ambivalent policy, it had an obvious weakness in that there were no signs that the majority of those who actually participated in the frontier advance were willing to accept the Indians as equals and fellow Americans. To do so would of course have meant that the Indians would have had to retain at least sufficient land to farm. Jefferson argued that this would be done and would be the means of welding Americans and Indians together. But the settlers of Georgia, Tennessee, Ohio, and Indiana gave no indication that they looked upon the Indians as brothers, only that they wanted to take all the available good land. To the frontiersmen the Indians were an obstacle, as the terrain or natural hazards were obstacles. They wanted to drive out or annihilate them, not perpetuate them on the land.

The Coming of War

X

IN INDIAN RELATIONS, as in European affairs, President James Madison was bequeathed a host of problems by his predecessors. Even had he been a more forceful executive it is difficult to see how he could have achieved a happy result, and as it was he merely continued and echoed the Indian policies of Jefferson. In his Inaugural Address of March 4, 1809, Madison stated that it was his intention "to carry on the benevolent plans which have been so meritoriously applied to the conversion of our aboriginal neighbors from the degradation and wretchedness of savage life to a participation of the improvements of which the human mind and manners are susceptible in a civilized state."[1] Madison demonstrated no noticeable change of views in the next two years. In his First Annual Message of November 29, 1809, he wrote: "With our Indian neighbors, the just and benevolent system continued toward them has also preserved peace, and is more and more advancing habits favorable to their civilization and happiness." And even as late as December 1810, after Tecumseh had visited Amherstburg and told British Agent Matthew Elliott that all was ready for war, Madison was able to say in his Second Annual Message: "With the Indian tribes also the peace and friendship of the United States are found to be so eligible that the general disposition to preserve both continues to gain strength." [2] By December 1810 Madison had ample reason to believe otherwise.

South of the Ohio Madison was faced with traditional problems at the beginning of his presidency—particularly the troublesome question of illegal intrusion upon Indian lands. In March 1809 acting Secretary of War John Smith informed Cherokee Agent Meigs that intruders on Cherokee and Chickasaw lands could be moved by military force if necessary. In accordance with these orders Meigs did have the settlers removed from the lands of both these tribes.[3]

But complaints of encroachment continued. In the winter of 1809-1810 the new Secretary of War, William Eustis, had to enjoin his southern agents to try to conciliate the Indians on this question. In November 1809 Major James Neely, the new agent to the Chickasaws, was asked to give formal notice to the intruders on Cherokee lands that unless they abandoned their possessions by the time of the next planting they would be removed by military force. In the same month the Secretary of War asked Benjamin Hawkins to use "every reasonable and practicable mode within the limits of the Law" to prevent future aggressions on Creek territory. Hawkins was ordered to warn the intruders on Creek lands that they would have to abandon their settlements or be removed by military force. The President also sent a message to the Creek National Council assuring the Creeks that the government did not condone the activities of illegal intruders. "Your Land is your own," wrote the President, "Nobody can make it smaller without your consent." To the Creek plea that they were poor, Madison replied in the style of Jefferson, telling them to fence in their lands, plough as much as they could, raise corn, hogs, and cattle, and have their women spin and weave. This would give them food and clothing, argued Madison, and they would live comfortably.[4]

The news from Chickasaw country abounded in accounts of

intrusions and Indian complaints. It was reliably reported that some four to five thousand settlers had passed beyond the Indian boundary and were determined to remain there unless removed by force. Many of these were on the lands north of the Tennessee River.[5] Even though the United States had tried to bring some order into the western advance by organizing repeated cessions and creating boundary lines which for the time being were supposed to be inviolate, the government was never able to stem the illegal advance. Settlers crossed the boundary line to obtain choice lands, and the government never mustered sufficient military force to prevent the intrusions. Yet, in the spring of 1810, the Secretary of War told Agent James Neely that the President was taking measures to correct the situation. The pledge was of little use, for in the following months and years the problem continued so that as late as December 1811, when the United States was preparing for war against England, the Secretary of War was still writing to Neely to tell him that troops would be sent to Chickasaw country to remove the intruders.[6]

Though the government was fighting a losing battle to protect existing boundaries in the South until new official cessions had been made, the government itself in one respect continued to ask for privileges beyond the boundary line. As under Jefferson, the administration was constantly trying to establish roads through the Indian country. The Indians had continually resisted these efforts because they well knew that roads brought official mail carriers, travellers, ruffians, and the establishment of way stations, all of which helped to prepare the way for the next advance of the American frontier.

Resistance or not, Madison's Administration was determined to establish roads through the Indian country, and in 1810 and 1811 Indian resistance was simply pushed aside. The first intimations of the pressure of the future came in the spring of 1810 when the Secretary of War informed Meigs, Hawkins, and Dinsmoor that some of the inhabitants of Tennessee had applied for permission to travel through Cherokee, Choctaw, and Creek country for the purpose of trading with Mobile.[7] The agents were to attempt to make this possible in their different agencies. Though the Indians showed not the slightest enthusiasm for this project, plans went ahead with little regard for their wishes. In the fall of 1810 the Creeks objected to surveying parties being sent into the Indian country, but Creek consternation was not allowed to deter the government from its goal. In January 1811 Hawkins was told to impress upon the Creeks the importance of surveying a route from Highwassee to the Mobile. Eustis anticipated Creek approval for these surveying parties and told Hawkins to send the result of his talks with the Creeks as soon as possible, as the surveying parties should begin their task in May or early June. In fact, in writing to William Blount in February 1811, the Secretary of War discussed it as a *fait accompli*. He said Hawkins was to attend a Creek council in March to explain the reasons for government explorations within their boundaries "and to inform them" that the survey would begin in the coming season.[8]

Though the proposed road from Tennessee to the Mobile was for the time being the most important extension of communications beyond the Indian boundaries, the Chickasaws also were under pressure in this regard in the spring of 1811. Kentucky asked the federal government to obtain Chickasaw permission to open a road from the site of the Chickasaw agency to Widow Runnole's ferry on the Tennessee River. Once again the Secretary of War acted as though the Indians would be as enthusiastic as the Americans over a proposed road. He explained to Agent Neelly that the road would be of great benefit to the United States and the benefits to the Chickasaws, he said, "leave no doubt of their readiness to grant such permission." Neelly was to ascertain the sentiments of the chiefs and get permission for the road and way stations. Like the other tribes the Chickasaws had no enthusiasm for the intrusion of a road, and on May 25 the Secretary of War told Neelly that he could pay five hundred dollars for such permission if the Indians demanded compensation. If they wanted still more, Neelly was to refer the request to the War Department.[9]

The spring of 1811 also brought renewed demands for a

further advance of the official boundary. The trans-Appalachian settlers and their governments were becoming impatient with the temporary hiatus in Indian cessions. Tennessee, Kentucky, and South Carolina were now all urging the federal government to secure the cession of Indian lands within those states, and both Tennessee and Kentucky were pressing for the establishment of communications through the Indian country, Tennessee being particularly desirous of establishing connections with the waters of the Mobile.[10]

The new pressure upon the government to obtain the cession of lands brought a renewed interest in the possibility of Indian emigration beyond the Mississippi River. This had first been brought up by Jefferson after the Louisiana Purchase, had been discussed again in regard to the Cherokees in Jefferson's second term, and had been brought up early in Madison's administration, again in regard to the same tribe. At that time Madison had shown no great enthusiasm and had suggested that a gradual migration rather than any mass movement would be preferable. Now, with the new pressure from the state of Tennessee, the Secretary of War revived the issue. In March 1811 Eustis asked Meigs to find out if the Cherokees would like to exchange their lands within the states of Tennessee and South Carolina for lands beyond the Mississippi. Eustis also again raised the question of a road from Tennessee to the Mobile (via the Tombigbee), saying that the government intended to open such a road and that, depending on the route, it might become expedient to obtain the consent of the Cherokees.[11]

The Secretary of War wrote to Neelly in March to inform him that the time was not distant when Chickasaw claims to lands within the states of Kentucky and Tennessee would have to be extinguished and that he must prepare the Chickasaw chiefs for such an event. As usual, the Secretary of War thought that the Indians could have little real reason to dispute the American desires. "It is desireable that the settlements within those States should be extended to the Mississippi," wrote Eustis, "and, as the lands in question are not used by, and are of no great value to the Chickasaws, it is expected that their title will be conveyed to the United States for the use of those States for a very moderate consideration." He also reminded Neelly of the plan to open a road from Tennessee to the Mobile and instructed him to obtain Chickasaw consent for that road by pointing out the roads and water courses were given by the "Great Spirit" for common use and that white roads and rivers were open to the red people. As the United States had acquired the navigation of the waters of the Mobile, argued Eustis, it had become necessary that the people of Tennessee have the use of the rivers and roads leading to the Bay of Mobile to transport their produce and receive articles they desired in return.[12]

The Secretary of War, in his bland assumption that the Indians would accept that what was good for the Americans was also good for them, received a shock in the early summer when news arrived that the Creeks had been unreceptive to the idea of the Tennessee-Mobile road as presented by Hawkins. "The answer of the creeks appears to be unreasonable, and is by no means satisfactory," wrote Eustis. "The rapid increase of the settlements above, makes it certain that the time is near at hand, when they must have roads, & use of the Water courses to the bay of Mobile." In this case even the usually fictitious freedom of choice for the Indians was abandoned, for the Creeks were given no option but to accept the proposed Tennessee-Mobile road. "It would give the President pain to do any act which would imply injustice to the creek nation," wrote Eustis, "but the White Inhabitants have their rights and their claims upon him as well as the Indians." Eustis concluded by telling Hawkins that it remained for the Creeks to reconsider, "and to give their consent." The alternative would be to "compel the Government to the use of means which it is desirous to avoid." [13]

But the government did not even wait for this forced reconsideration. In less than a month Eustis again wrote to Hawkins saying that since his previous letter the President had decided that a wagon road would be opened from the Tennessee River to Fort Stoddert (on the Mobile), and another from Fort Stoddert to Hawkins' station on the Flint River. Hawkins was to explain to the Creeks that consistent with a friendly disposition towards them and with a proper respect for their rights, the President had found it necessary in the interest of public service to have roads for the transportation of ordnance and military stores from one post to another. This same determination was now sent to Neelly in the Chickasaw agency. He was told by the Secretary of War that a road was to be opened from the Tennessee to the Mobile, that the road from the Tennessee to the Chickasaw agency would have to be marked out, and that his interpreter (who had previously balked at pressuring the Chickasaws into yielding this road) would either have to support the views of the government or be dismissed.[14]

Thus, in 1811 and 1812, despite Indian opposition, the United States opened roads in the Indian country. It was quite clearly demonstrated that boundary lines existed as long as they were convenient and helped to preserve peace and permit rapid settlement, but at the last instant, the Indian right to cede or not to cede, to grant or not to grant, was practically meaningless. Indian resistance could delay cession or a road, but could not ultimately prevent it. Normally, the pressure used to break down Indian refusal was a constant reiteration of requests, arguments, or bribery, but if a situation reached a stalemate, the government was prepared to proceed in spite of Indian refusal.

The roads went ahead, but not, for the time being, the cession of land. In spite of the desires of Kentucky and Tennessee, the Cherokees and the Chickasaws held on to their claims. Some Cherokees moved west of the Mississippi, but most stayed where they were, and some continued their efforts to adopt the ways of civilization; but as Kentucky and Tennessee expanded to the Mississippi and the populations of those states increased, the hopes of permanent, civilized homes for the Indians east of the Mississippi, regardless of what Jefferson had said, became more and more unlikely.

Good land was in ever-increasing demand, and the frontiers-men would not rest content while any of it remained in Indian hands. As the danger of war with England increased, the southern Indians could hope to retain their lands temporarily, but it was obvious that when peace returned, it would bring new demands for westward expansion.

There were almost hopeless problems in the North that Madison had inherited from his predecessor. In spite of Jefferson's assumptions that the process of civilization was succeeding and that the Indians were realizing the advantages of American ways, the northwest Indians were, in fact, almost ready for open resistance. Tecumseh and his brother the Prophet had gathered around them on the Tippecanoe a large band of dissident tribesmen, and Tecumseh had attempted to carry his influence far and wide over the Mississippi Valley. He argued for common ownership of Indian land—not merely the tribal ownership which Jefferson had been so keen to eliminate in favor of private property, but common ownership among all the tribes; no one tribe, stated Tecumseh, had the right to cede lands on its own behalf. This doctrine was a direct challenge to American policy since the 1790's by which everything possible had been done to imbue the Indians with the idea of private property, of their own, fenced, individual lands. If Tecumseh's plans succeeded, the United States would no longer be able to persuade individual chiefs to cede lands for some small consideration for themselves.

Also in opposition to American policy was the "nativistic" movement preached by the Prophet. The casting off of all white influence, white goods and white ideas, stood in direct contrast to the idea that what was best for the Indians was a rapid adoption of the whites' civilization. Since the 1790's arguments for private property and white mores had accompanied the demand for land; now Tecumseh's movement aimed at holding on to land and resisting the blandishments of the more comfortable and happy life.

In the Old Northwest and throughout the Mississippi Valley, Indian resistance was growing. The defeats of the 1790's had brought temporary peace, but now the Greenville line was collapsing, and the northwest Indians were ready to fight to resist the next stage in the advance of the American frontier. The new government showed no real sign that it recognized the imminent danger posed by this deterioration of relations and stiffening Indian resistance. Within six months of Madison's assumption of the presidency, the successive land acquisitions of Harrison, mostly carried on under Jefferson's presidency, reached their culmination in the Treaty of Fort Wayne. On July 15, 1809, the Secretary of War informed Harrison that the President had authorized and instructed him to take advantage of the most favorable opportunity for extinguishing Indian title to the lands lying to the east of the Wabash and adjoining to the south lands previously ceded by the Indians at the Treaty of Fort Wayne in 1803 and at Grouseland in 1805. Once again it was stated that the payment made should not exceed the rate previously given in that area for the purchase of Indian land. Harrison was instructed to negotiate with the chiefs of all nations who either had or pretended to have right to these lands.[15]

Harrison needed no additional prompting. With his usual enthusiasm he obtained the desired treaty—a treaty which was sure to raise the ire of those Indians who had been listening to the equally enthusiastic Tecumseh. The treaty was signed at Fort Wayne on September 30, 1809, with the Delawares, Potawatomis, Miamis, and Eel Rivers. Two additional cessions of southern Indiana land were now made by these Indians; one of these was directly north of the Vincennes cession, and the other in eastern Indiana directly adjoining the strip of southeastern Indiana that had been ceded at the Treaty of Greenville. A month later, at Vincennes, the Weas gave their full assent to the Treaty of Fort Wayne. On December 9 the Kickapoos also agreed to the treaty and ceded another small tract of land west of the Wabash to the United States.[16]

The treaty of Fort Wayne flouted the wishes of the growing Indian resistance in the Old Northwest. Though the government had insisted that it was honoring the Treaty of Greenville and only obtaining land with the full consent of the

Indians, many of the Indians considered that the Greenville treaty had been broken by the United States. Large cessions of land had been made on the Indian side of the Greenville line, and the hostile Indians considered that these had been achieved through undue pressure and without the full consent of the tribes. Those Indians who had gathered around Tecumseh, on the Tippecanoe, were not prepared to see their land in the Old Northwest whittled away by cession after cession. After the Treaty of Fort Wayne, tension in the Old Northwest increased greatly, and Harrison constantly reported the danger of war. He tended to blame Indian hostility on the activities of British agents, but though it was true that the British at Amherstburg were attempting to win Indian allegiance, the basic cause of Indian hostility was the advance of the American frontier and the disappearance of Indian hopes that the Greenville line would permanently divide the Indians and Americans.[17]

With the Treaty of Fort Wayne it now became obvious that the immediate problem in the Northwest was the maintenance of peace and tightening control over the cessions that had already been made rather than obtaining new cessions. In the spring and summer of 1810 the government weighed the possibilities of establishing a post within the new cession, north of Vincennes on the Wabash, and of marking the boundaries, but became apprehensive by news of increased Indian hostility. Finally, in October 1810, Eustis informed Harrison that the President had decided that it was not expedient to establish a new post or run the boundaries at that time. Eustis suggested that in the spring of 1811 a favorable opportunity would present itself to establish a strong post and "display a respectable force on the Wabash," this being the only language which would be understood by the Prophet and his adherents. The surest way to secure good behavior from the Prophet and his brother would be to make them prisoners, suggested Eustis, but at the present time it was important to maintain peace, and Harrison should consider this a primary object.[18]

Though Eustis advised caution, Harrison was not loath to

press ahead with further demands for land. In December 1810 he suggested that more Indian land titles should be extinguished, but was advised that the President did not think it expedient to adopt such measures at that time. Moreover, Eustis felt that some future arrangement might become necessary to quiet possible discontent over the Treaty of Fort Wayne.[19]

Eustis was right in his caution, for in 1811 Indian relations in the Old Northwest approached a crisis. From the Illinois Territory, which had been created in 1809, came news of several murders and a state of general alarm. Harrison also reported widespread discontent, and in July Eustis informed him that some five hundred men were descending the Ohio from Pittsburgh to reinforce him. Moreover, he told Harrison that he could call out the militia in case it might be necessary, "or expedient," to attack the Prophet and his followers. "If the prophet should commence, or seriously threaten, hostilities," wrote Eustis, "he ought to be attacked, provided the force under your command is sufficient to insure success." [20]

This freedom to attack was modified three days later, presumably on the direct instructions of the President. "I have been particularly instructed by the President," wrote Eustis, "to communicate his earnest desire that peace may, if possible, be preserved with the Indians." Eustis emphasized, however, that this did not mean that the frontier should not be defended, and if necessary, the Prophet attacked; however, by September attack had once again become the policy of the Secretary of War. He suggested to Harrison (specifying that his ideas could be observed or departed from as Harrison thought best) that on approaching the Prophet, Harrison should order him to disperse his force. If he refused, then he should be attacked.[21]

Harrison was certainly given all the authority he needed to attack the encampment on the Tippecanoe, and in October he advanced his force northwards from Vincennes toward Prophetstown. Tecumseh was not there to meet him, for in the summer he had gone on a visit to the southern tribes in order to enlist their support for his confederacy. Harrison advanced to within a few miles of Prophetstown and encamped. The Indians did not wait for his next move, but attacked him at dawn on the following day; after a sharp clash the Indians fled from the field. It was not a crushing victory for the Americans, for losses were probably about even, but Tecumseh's hopes of a solid confederacy were given a fatal blow. Harrison was to reap great advantages from this victory (which had none of the decisiveness of Wayne's), and on December 11 Eustis wrote to congratulate him "on the successful and important issue of a conflict unparalleled in our history." Throughout his tenure as Secretary of War, Eustis had shown little understanding of Indian affairs. His opinion of Tippecanoe was that "it is presumed that the effects of this defeat will be experienced in a return of the Indians to their former friendly dispositions, and in a prevention of future aggressions." This optimism was completely misplaced, for Tippecanoe was followed by sporadic warfare on the frontiers of the Old Northwest— warfare which was soon to blend into the War of 1812.[22]

In the winter of 1811-1812 the United States had at last decided to declare war on England, and after months of debate, did so on June 18, 1812. By that time many of the Indians of the Old Northwest were quite ready to fight for the British, another group were to remain neutral, but very few were to fight on the American side. This stemmed partly from the efforts of British agents who from 1807 had worked hard to ensure that the British would have Indian support if war broke out, but primarily from Indian fear of the American frontier advance. The Indians knew that the British were using them for their own devices, but they had little choice. They were rapidly losing control of the Old Northwest, and they took the opportunity of the War of 1812 to fight another war in their own defense. In the months directly proceeding the War of 1812 the American government attempted to win the allegiance of the Indians, but by then it was too late. The Indians remembered the cessions from 1783 to 1812, not the promises of friendly relations in the future.

Conclusion

WITH THE OUTBREAK of the War of 1812 the first phase of United States Indian policy came to an end. In the war itself Indian policy had to consist either of fighting those Indians who joined the British or persuading any who were doubtful to remain neutral. After the War of 1812 the obvious failure of the process of assimilation over most of the eastern half of the Mississippi Valley quickly brought a policy of Indian removal with a new goal not of union, but of the separation of whites and Indians. After 1812, it was not until after the Civil War that the American government again based its policy so clearly on a doctrine of assimilation.

The history of American relations with the Indians in the years from 1783 to 1812 is sometimes written as though there was no coherent policy, with the government merely chasing after the settlers, as though they were in competition, and defining and defending boundary lines to protect the Indians from the onrushing frontiersmen. This view ignores the extent to which the United States Government attempted to work out a coherent policy to deal with the problem of expansion over territory occupied by an aboriginal population.

In the first years after the Revolution, in spite of warnings to the contrary, the Confederation Government attempted a policy of naked power. From 1783 to 1786 it was assumed that the land to the Mississippi was solely American and that the Indians were only pawns to be moved when and where the United States Government desired. This direct approach failed on two grounds: The first was that it required money and military strength, neither of which the Confederation possessed; the second was that simple conquest of the Indians required the elimination of moral considerations and a nonchalance to external or internal criticism on these grounds. Few nations are willing to assume this attitude and few have been more sensitive in this regard than the post-Revolutionary United States. The ideas of undertaking a great experiment in republican government, of setting an example to Europe, of showing that nations as well as individuals could live by moral standards, all affected the leaders of post-Revolutionary United States. The policy of ignoring any Indian rights quickly brought qualms to those who thought that the extermination of the Indians would besmirch the honor of the new nation.

Under the pressure of these problems of money, military force, and conscience, the United States moved to a more elaborate policy in the years after 1786—a policy by which United States leaders thought that expansion would be facilitated. An essential change was the return to the British and colonial practice of acknowledging Indian right of soil; a right which would have to be purchased by the United States in formal treaty. It was hoped that formal purchases of land would satisfy the Indians and that definite boundary lines would be established which the United States would guarantee to protect against its own citizens thus preventing incidents and wars. To effect this a series of trade and intercourse acts were passed which attempted to maintain a strict control over the American frontier advance.

Though it was hoped that the Indians would be appeased by the purchase of land and by federal protection of Indian boundaries, there was no intention to give up future expansion. It was expected that as the Indians adjacent to boundary lines found game and their fellow tribesmen disappearing, they would certainly consent to future purchases and new boundary lines. This policy was further elaborated in the 1790's as the concept of bringing civilization to the Indians gained ground. Though it was hoped that a policy of purchase rather than confiscation of land and the protection of Indian boundaries would make expansion easier and prevent extensive wars, it would still not solve the problem of a troubled conscience; the Indians would still be dwindling in numbers and would, presumably, eventually disappear. The United States could expect every material advantage from advancing across the Mississippi Valley (its possession would ensure her future status as a nation), but as a country which prided itself on its superiority to the decadent powers of Europe, it was galling to be placed in the position of exterminating the aboriginal owners of that rich area. To bring the blessings of civilization would give a perfect justification for the American advance. Taking land could become a blessing for those from whom it was taken, and American expansion would benefit not only the Americans, but also those who stood in their path.

This policy, which reached its peak under Jefferson, made insufficient allowance for the desires of the states, the settlers, or the Indians. In the South the states themselves flouted the orderly advance of the federal government, despite the desperate attempts of the central government to take Indian relations into its own hands. American frontiersmen along the entire length of the American frontier were not content to wait for an orderly advance; they wanted to be first into the choicest lands and often ignored the trade and intercourse acts. Though the government attempted to stop them, it usually at the last instant became a question of whether to turn extensive military force against its own citizens or against the Indians. Though military force was used occasionally against American citizens, the idea was so unpalatable that the government preferred to fight the Indians.

But the fatal flaw in the whole policy was a misjudgement of the Indians themselves; a misjudgement that perhaps stemmed from an unwillingness to face reality. The Indians did not want to yield their lands either to conquest or by purchase and were prepared to fight rather than accept the constant requests for sales of land. Rather than the land beyond each boundary slipping easily and quietly into American hands, each major advance brought bitter resentment and Indian hostilities; they resented forced purchase as they had resented the land appropriation of the years immediately following the Revolution. Moreover, the bringing of civilization was no solution. Though this was not realized in the post-Revolutionary period, acculturation was a long and incredibly difficult process. And, of course, even where limited success was achieved—notably among the Cherokees—it was quite obvious that whatever the desires of the government to maintain the good reputation of the nation, the frontiersmen were more interested in the Indian giving up his land than learning to farm it.

The Americans in these years from 1783 to 1812 foreshadowed the arguments of their descendents in the mid-nineteenth century when they attempted to place their expansion on firm moral foundations. At this time it was the Indians who were to receive the benefits of American civilization; later it was to be the Mexicans or even the Canadians, still later the Hawaiians or the Filipinos. In this endeavor to give expansion a moral basis the Americans were not, of course, unique. Western Europeans have always tended to justify their advance over large areas of the world in terms of spreading civilization—whether it be to the American Indian, the Maori, or the Zulu. In these post-Revolutionary years the young United States faced a typical nineteenth-century dilemma and attempted to solve it in a way which would benefit both the national interest and the national honor. The attempt at peaceful expansion—an expansion which Indian inhabitants of the Mississippi Valley would welcome—failed. But there seems no reason to believe that any policy other than a total abandonment of the Mississippi Valley to the Indians would have succeeded. The problem could perhaps have been dealt with more realistically, but there seems no reason to believe that it could have been solved.

Notes

Chapter 1: Establishing a Policy, 1783-1784

1 The Treaty of September 3, 1783, is in Hunter Miller, ed. *Treaties and Other International Acts of the United States of America* (Washington, 1931-   ), II, 151-57. Indian relations during the Revolution are considered in Walter H. Mohr, *Federal Indian Relations, 1774-1788* (Philadelphia, 1933).

2 Merrill Jensen, *The New Nation: A History of the United States During the Confederation, 1781-1789* (New York, 1950), pp. 67-68; Worthington C. Ford, *et. al.*, eds. *Journals of the Continental Congress, 1774-1789* (34 vols., Washington, 1904-1937), XXIV, 264. See also Benjamin Lincoln to Brigadier-General William Irvine, May 3, 1783, Consul W. Butterfield, ed. *Washington-Irvine Correspondence* (Madison, Wis., 1882), p. 188,

and Clarence M. Burton, ed. "Ephraim Douglass and His Times," in *Magazine of History with Notes and Queries,* extra numbers, III, 10 (New York, 1910), 50-61.

³ For American finance in these years see E. James Ferguson, *The Power of the Purse: A History of American Public Finance, 1776-1790* (Chapel Hill, 1961), and for the development of American land policy, Payson J. Treat, *The National Land System, 1785-1820* (New York, 1910).

⁴ Knox to Washington, April 17, 1783, Henry Knox Papers, XII, 101, Massachusetts Historical Society, microfilm in State Historical Society, Madison, Wisconsin; Washington to the President of Congress, June 17, 1783, John C. Fitzpatrick, ed. *The Writings of George Washington* (39 vols., Washington, 1931-1944), XXVII, 17-18.

⁵ Schuyler to the President of Congress, July 29, 1783, Papers of the Continental Congress, 1774-1789, Item 153, III, 601-607, National Archives, Washington, D. C.; also *ibid.,* 593-95, Schuyler to President of Congress, September 21, 1782.

⁶ *Journals of the Continental Congress,* XXIV, 501, n. 1. The committee consisted of James Duane, Richard Peters, Daniel Carroll, Benjamin Hawkins, and Arthur Lee.

⁷ Washington to Duane, September 7, 1783, Fitzpatrick, ed. *Writings of Washington,* XXVII, 133-40.

⁸ *Journals of the Continental Congress,* XXV, 602. The best discussion of federal efforts to create a separate Indian country is Francis P. Prucha, *American Indian Policy in the Formative Years: The Indian Trade and Intercourse Acts, 1790-1834* (Cambridge, Mass., 1962).

⁹ The report and resolutions of October 15, 1783, are in *Journals of the Continental Congress,* XXV, 681-93.

¹⁰ The state of Indian affairs in the South was referred on October 16 to a committee consisting of Benjamin Hawkins, James Madison, Richard Beresford, James McHenry, and James Tilton. Before the report of this committee was delivered in the spring of 1784, Hawkins, Madison, McHenry, and Tilton had been replaced by Jeremiah Townley Chase, Thomas Jefferson, Richard Dobbs Spaight, and Jacob Read. See *Journals of the Continental Congress,* XXV, 692, n. 1. The report of May 28, 1784, which was first read on April 19, *ibid.,* XXVII, 453-65.

¹¹ For cession of western land claims from 1781 to 1802 see Treat, *National Land System,* pp. 1-13, 340-69.

Chapter 2: The Policy in Practice, 1784-1786

¹ The five original commissioners were George Rogers Clark, Oliver Wolcott, Nathaniel Greene, Richard Butler, and Stephen Higginson, *Journals of the Continental Congress,* XXVI, 124-25. Clark, Greene, and Higginson declined their appointments, and Benjamin Lincoln and Arthur Lee were appointed in their places,

ibid., 282. See also the Virginia delegates to Benjamin Harrison, May 13, 1784, Edmund C. Burnett, ed. *Letters of Members of the Continental Congress* (8 vols., Washington, 1921-1938), VII, 525, and Henry S. Manley, *The Treaty of Fort Stanwix, 1784* (Rome, N.Y., 1932), p. 49.

2 *Journals of the Continental Congress*, XXVI, 123, 153-54, 238.

3 Manley, *Treaty of Fort Stanwix*, pp. 28-29, 51, and Hugh Hastings, ed. *The Public Papers of George Clinton* (10 vols., New York, 1899-1914), VIII, 323.

4 Hastings, ed. *Public Papers of Clinton*, VIII, 323-25, 327-28.

5 *Ibid.*, 332-35; Manley, *Treaty of Fort Stanwix*, p. 54.

6 Hastings, ed. *Public Papers of Clinton*, VIII, 337-40; also Butler and Lee to Oliver Wolcott, August 20, 1784, Burnett, ed. *Letters of Members of the Continental Congress*, VII, 584, n. 3.

7 Minutes of the New York council with the Indians are in Hastings, ed. *Public Papers of Clinton*, VIII, 349-79.

8 The minutes of the Fort Stanwix Treaty Council, October 3-October 21, 1784, are in Neville B. Craig, ed. *The Olden Time* (2 vols., Pittsburgh, 1848, reprinted Cincinnati, 1876), II, 406-28. The treaty is in *Statutes at Large of the United States of America* (Boston, 1853), VII, 15-16.

9 For the journey of the commissioners to the West see the journal of Arthur Lee, in Craig, ed. *The Olden Time*, II, 334-44. The minutes of the Fort McIntosh Treaty Council are in the Timothy Pickering Papers, LIX, 119-26, Massachusetts Historical Society, Cambridge, Mass., and the treaty is in *Statutes at Large*, VII, 16-18.

10 *Journals of the Continental Congress*, XXVIII, 66-67, 125-26, 172-73, 330-33, 460-62, 486-87.

11 Message to the Chippewas and Ottawas, July 31, 1785, and to the chiefs of the Wyandots, August 3, 1785, *Michigan Pioneer and Historical Collections* (40 vols., Lansing, 1877-1929), XXIV, 21-22.

12 For British policy in the Old Northwest after 1783 see A. L. Burt, *The United States, Great Britain, and British North America, from the Revolution to the Establishment of Peace after the War of 1812* (New Haven, 1940), pp. 82-105, and Randolph C. Downes, *Council Fires on the Upper Ohio: A Narrative of Indian Affairs in the Upper Ohio Valley until 1795* (Pittsburgh, 1940), pp. 277-309. As early as September 1783 the British told the Indians they were still the sole proprietors of land northwest of the Ohio River boundary established at Fort Stanwix in 1768, see *Michigan Pioneer and Historical Collections*, XX, 176-77.

13 See Captain John Doughty to Henry Knox, October 21, 1785, Consul W. Butterfield, ed. *Journal of Capt. Jonathan Heart . . . to Which Is Added the Dickinson-Harmar Correspondence of 1784-1785* (Albany, 1885), pp. 88-91, and Knox to Charles Thomson, November 24, 1785, and enclosures, Papers of the Continental Congress, Item 150, I, 103-131.

[14] The proceedings of the treaty can be followed in the journal of Richard Butler, in Craig, ed. *The Olden Time,* II, 433-64, 481-525, 529-31. The treaty is in *Statutes at Large,* VII, 26-27; the boundary was drawn from the forks of the Great Miami westward to the River de la Panse (Wildcat Creek), and down that river to the Wabash. For the Huron, Ottawa, Chippewa, and Potawatomi reply to the invitation to the treaty see their message to the Americans, September 20, 1785, in Draper Manuscripts, 23U27, State Historical Society, Madison, Wisconsin.

[15] For Shawnee dissatisfaction with the treaty at the mouth of the Great Miami see *Michigan Pioneer and Historical Collections,* XXIV, 25-26. For reactions of Congress and relations on this matter with Virginia see James Manning to Hezekiah Smith, May 17, 1786; Rufus King to Elbridge Gerry, June 8, 1786; Secretary of Congress to Patrick Henry, July 3, 1786; in Burnett, ed. *Letters of the Members of the Continental Congress,* VIII, 362-63, 384, 399; *Journals of the Continental Congress,* XXX, 373-79, XXXI, 656-58, 891-93, 916-18. For increase of Indian depredations in summer of 1786 see Josiah Harmar to Henry Knox, July 12, 1786, William H. Smith, ed. *The St. Clair Papers* (2 vols., Cincinnati, 1882), II, 14-15, and W. North to George Rogers Clark, August 7, 1786, in Northwest Territory Collection, William Henry Smith Memorial Library, Indianapolis. The expeditions of Clark and Logan are considered in Leonard C. Helderman, "The Northwest Expedition of Clark," *Mississippi Valley Historical Review,* XXV (1938), 317-34; also *Michigan Pioneer and Historical Collections,* XXIV, 34-39, and Harmar to Knox, November 15, 1786, Smith, ed. *St. Clair Papers,* II, 18-19.

[16] *American State Papers, Indian Affairs* (2 vols., Washington, 1832-1834), I, 8-9; also *Michigan Pioneer and Historical Collections,* XI, 470-72.

[17] For the state of Franklin see Samuel C. Williams, *History of the Lost State of Franklin* (New York, 1933), and Thomas P. Abernethy, *From Frontier to Plantation in Tennessee: A Study in Frontier Democracy* (Chapel Hill, 1932). Problems with the Cherokees are dealt with in Randolph C. Downes, "Cherokee American Relations in the Upper Tennessee Valley, 1776-1791," East Tennessee Historical Society, *Publications,* VIII (1936), 35-53. Spanish border policy is treated in Arthur P. Whitaker, *The Spanish-American Frontier: 1783-1795* (Boston, 1927, and in John W. Caughey, *McGillivray of the Creeks* (Norman, Okla., 1938).

[18] *Journals of the Continental Congress,* XXVII, 550-53; also Hugh Williamson to Alexander Martin, July 5, September 30, 1784, Burnett, ed. *Letters of the Members of the Continental Congress,* VII, 562-64, 593-98.

[19] *Journals of the Continental Congress,* XXVII, 464, n. 1. The report was referred to Samuel Hardy, William Houstown, Jacob Read, Hugh Williamson, and Samuel Holton on December 15, 1784.

[20] *Ibid.,* XXVIII, 118-20.

[21] When the report was recommitted on March 10, David Howell replaced Read, *ibid.*, XXVIII, 134, n. 2. The revised report of March 11 is *ibid.*, XXVIII, 136-37.

[22] *Ibid.*, XXVIII, 138-39, 159-62, 195. The five commissioners were Benjamin Hawkins, Daniel Carroll, William Peery, Andrew Pickens, and Joseph Martin, *ibid.*, XXVIII, 183-84. Carroll declined his appointment, and on May 16 Lachlin M'Intosh was appointed in his place, *ibid.*, XXVIII, 347-48, 362.

[23] See Samuel G. McLendon, *History of the Public Domain of Georgia* (Atlanta, 1924), and Arthur P. Whitaker, "The Muscle Shoals Speculation," *Mississippi Valley Historical Review*, XIII (1926), 365-86.

[24] See *American State Papers, Indian Affairs*, I, 19-20, 23; Caughey, *McGillivray of the Creeks*, pp. 24-27, 64-67 (documents). Georgia pressure on the Creeks in this period is discussed in Randolph C. Downes, ("Creek-American Relations, 1782-1790," *Georgia Historical Quarterly*, XXI (1937), 142-84.

[25] See R. S. Cotterill, *The Southern Indians: The Story of the Civilized Tribes Before Removal* (Norman, Okla., 1954), pp. 57-67 and Williams, *Lost State of Franklin*, pp. 77-79.

[26] McGillivray to Andrew Pickens, September 5, 1785; United States Commissioners to Charles Thomson, November 17, 1785; *American State Papers, Indian Affairs*, I, 16, 17-18; also Caughey, *McGillivray of the Creeks*, pp. 28, 98, n. 46; and Hawkins to McGillivray, January 8, 1786, *ibid.*, pp. 101-102; Merritt B. Pound, *Benjamin Hawkins—Indian Agent* (Athens, Ga., 1951), pp. 39-45.

[27] This Georgia treaty with the Creeks is printed in *American State Papers, Indian Affairs*, I, 17.

[28] The minutes of the Hopewell Treaty with the Cherokees are in *ibid.*, 40-43. See also the correspondence regarding the treaty (including Blount's protest) *ibid.*, 38-39, 44. For Blount's role in these proceedings see William H. Masterson, *William Blount* (Baton Rouge, 1954), pp. 102-106. The treaty itself is in *Statutes at Large*, VII, 18-21.

[29] See *American State Papers, Indian Affairs*, I, 49-52; Masterson, *Blount*, 107-109; Pound, *Hawkins*, 50-51. The treaties are in *Statutes at Large*, VII, 21-26.

[30] *Journals of the Continental Congress*, XXVIII, 297.

[31] For the Shoulderbone Treaty see *American State Papers, Indian Affairs*, I, 23-24; Caughey, *McGillivray of the Creeks*, pp. 30-32, 139-41; Cotterill, *Southern Indians*, pp. 72-73; for the Cherokee Treaty see Williams, *Lost State of Franklin*, pp. 102-103.

Chapter 3: A New Start, 1786-1789

[1] *Journals of the Continental Congress*, XXX, 286-87, 396-97. The Committee consisted of James Monroe, William Samuel Johnson, Rufus King, John Kean, and Charles Pinckney.

[2] *Ibid.,* pp. 346-47.

[3] The committee to draft this ordinance had been appointed on June 6 and consisted of Charles Pinckney, James Monroe, and Rufus King, *ibid.,* XXX, 332. For the presentation of the report, discussion on it, and its final adoption see *ibid.,* XXX, 368-72, 413-19, 420-21, 424-28; XXXI, 485, 488-93.

[4] See above pp. 23-24; also Knox to Stephen Higginson, October 22, 1786; Jonathan Swan to Knox, October 26, 1786; David Cook to Knox, November 14, 1786; Knox to Colonel Wordsworth, October 22, 1786; Henry Knox Papers, XIX, 31, 32, 35, 51.

[5] *Journals of the Continental Congress,* XXXI, 891-93. The Board of Treasury reported on October 21 and recommended that $500,000 be raised through a loan. Congress agreed to this, *ibid.,* XXXI, 893-95.

[6] *Ibid.,* 916-18.

[7] Jay to Jefferson, December 14, 1786, Julian P. Boyd, ed. *The Papers of Thomas Jefferson* (Princeton, N. J., 1950-   ), X, 596-99.

[8] This committee, consisting of William Irvine, William Samuel Johnson, James Madison, Benjamin Hawkins, and Egbert Benson, was appointed on February 13, 1787, *Journals of the Continental Congress,* XXXII, 45. Their report of February 20 is *ibid.,* XXXII, 66-69.

[9] Knox to Winthrop Sargent, March 2, April 15, 1787, Henry Knox Papers.

[10] Clarence E. Carter, ed. *The Territorial Papers of the United States (Washington,* 1934-   ), II, 31-35.

[11] The resolution of April 23, 1784, is in *Journals of the Continental Congress,* XXVI, 274-79.

[12] The Northwest Ordinance is in Carter, ed. *Territorial Papers,* II, 39-50; see also *Journals of the Continental Congress,* XXXII, 334-43.

[13] *Journals of the Continental Congress,* XXXIII, 385; also William Blount to John Gray Blount, July 19, 1787, Burnett, ed. *Letters of the Members of the Continental Congress,* VIII, 624, and above pp. 23-24.

[14] *Journals of the Continental Congress,* XXXIII, 385-91.

[15] *Ibid.,* XXXII, 365-69.

[16] *Ibid.,* XXXIII, 410-11.

[17] *Ibid.,* 454-63.

[18] Knox's report of July 21 had been referred to this committee, which consisted of Nathan Dane, Benjamin Hawkins, John Kean, William Irvine, and Edward Carrington. The committee's report is *ibid.,* XXXIII, 477-81.

[19] *Ibid.,* XXXIII, 611-12, 665-66, 696. The difficulties of Congress on this matter were well expressed two days later by James Madison when he wrote "a Treaty with the Indians is on the anvil as a supplemental provision for the W. Country. It is not certain however that any thing will be done as it involves money, and we shall have on the floors nine States one more day only." James

Madison to Edmund Randolph, October 7, 1787, Burnett, ed. *Letters of the Members of the Continental Congress,* VIII, 655.

[20] See Benjamin H. Hibbard, *A History of the Public Land Policies* (New York, 1924), pp. 41-55, and Treat, *National Land System,* pp. 44-55. Also Carter, ed. *Territorial Papers,* II, 54-56, 70-71, 74-76, 80-84.

[21] See Richard Henry Lee to Washington, October 11, 1787; William Grayson to James Monroe, October 22, 1787; Burnett, ed. *Letters of the Members of the Continental Congress,* VIII, 656-57, 659; also *ibid.,* 629-32, 642-44, 660-61.

[22] See Carter, ed. *Territorial Papers,* II, 6-9, 12-18; also Thomas Donaldson, *The Public Domain* (Washington, 1884), pp. 232-34.

[23] Carter, ed. *Territorial Papers,* II, 78-79.

[24] See St. Clair to Knox, January 27, 1788, *ibid.,* II, 89-91, and St. Clair to Knox, March 14, 1788, Smith, ed. *St. Clair Papers,* II, 43.

[25] Report of the Secretary at War, March 31, 1788, Carter, ed. *Territorial Papers,* II, 100-102.

[26] *Journals of the Continental Congress,* XXXIV, 124-26.

[27] *Ibid.,* XXXIV, 285.

[28] Additional Instructions to St. Clair, July 2, 1788, Carter, ed. *Territorial Papers,* II, 117-18.

[29] St. Clair to Knox, July 16, 1788, *ibid.,* II, 130-32; *Journals of the Continental Congress,* XXXIV, 411-14.

[30] For some of these difficulties see William L. Stone, *Life of Joseph Brant* (2 vols., New York, 1838), II, 273-79; Brant to Richard Butler, July 8, 1788, Smith, ed. *St. Clair Papers,* II, 60-61; also Papers of the Continental Congress, no. 150, III, 277-78, 281-83, 285-87.

[31] See Brant to Patrick Langan, October 7, 1788, Stone, *Life of Brant,* II, 277-79.

[32] See Brant to St. Clair, November 19, 1788, with enclosed speech from the Six Nations, in Appendix to the Minutes of the Treaty of Fort Harmar, 1789, in Wayne Manuscripts, Indian Treaties, G, 24-29, Historical Society of Pennsylvania, Philadelphia.

[33] St. Clair to the Nations lately assembled at the Miami [Maumee] River, November 24, 1788, *ibid.,* 30-38; Six Nations to St. Clair, November 30, 1788, *ibid.,* 38-43; also St. Clair to Knox, December 3, 13, 1788, Smith, ed. *St. Clair Papers,* II, 99-100, 106-107.

[34] The proceedings of the Fort Harmar Treaty council are in Draper Manuscripts, 23U75-142. See also Appendix to the minutes of the Treaty of Fort Harmar, 1789, Wayne Manuscripts, Indian Treaties, G, 1-44, Historical Society of Pennsylvania, and "Military Journal of Major Ebeneezer Denny," in *Memoirs of the Historical Society of Pennsylvania,* VII (Philadelphia, 1860), 331-34.

[35] *Statutes at Large,* VII, 28-29.

[36] *Ibid.,* VII, 33-34.

[37] St. Clair to Washington, May 2, 1788, Carter, ed. *Territorial*

Papers, II, 191-93; see also St. Clair to Knox, January 18, 1789, Smith, ed. *St. Clair Papers,* II, 108-109.

38 For fears of war see Madison to Jefferson, October 24, Nov. 1, 1787; John Jay to Jefferson, November 3, 1787; Boyd, ed. *Jefferson Papers,* XI, 270-84, 316-17. Proceedings of Congress are in *Journals of the Continental Congress,* XXXIII, 707-11.

39 The May 26 report is in *Journals of the Continental Congress,* XXXIV, 182-83; July 18 report *ibid.,* XXXIV, 342-44.

40 *Ibid.,* 362-66, 368-71, 476-79. For actions of Franklin and others against the Cherokees see also Richard Winn to Knox, August 5, 1788; Joseph Martin to Knox, August 23, 1788; Justices of Court of Abbeville County to the people living on Nolichucky, French Broad, and Holston, July 9, 1788; Papers of the Continental Congress, Item 150, III, 369-70, 361-63, 349-52.

Chapter 4: The Aims of the New Government

1 *Annals of the Congress of the United States, 1789-1824* (42 vols., Washington, 1834-1856), 1 Congress, 1 Session, pp. 39-41.

2 This report of June 15, 1789, is in *American State Papers, Indian Affairs,* I, 12-14.

3 Report of July 7, 1789, is *ibid.,* 52-54.

4 James D. Richardson, *A Compilation of the Messages and Papers of the Presidents, 1789-1897* (10 vols., Washington, 1896-1907) I, 59. In the summer of 1789 Washington was collecting information from all possible sources in an effort to determine the correct policy to be pursued towards the Indians, see Washington to James Jackson, July 22, 1789, Fitzpatrick, ed. *Writings of Washington,* XXX, 358.

5 Richardson, ed. *Messages and Papers of the Presidents,* I, 104-105.

6 *Ibid.,* I, 125-27 (November 6), 122 (March 23).

7 See Knox to Captain Alexander Trueman, April 3, 1792, *American State Papers, Indian Affairs,* I, 229-30; Knox to Putnam, May 22, 1792, Rowena Buell, ed. *Memoirs of Rufus Putnam and Certain Official Papers and Correspondence* (Boston, 1903), pp. 257-67; Knox to Wayne, January 5, 1793, Richard C. Knopf, ed. *Anthony Wayne, a Name in Arms; Soldier, Diplomat, Defender of Expansion Westward of a Nation: The Wayne-Knox-Pickering-McHenry Correspondence* (Pittsburgh, 1960), pp. 164-67.

8 This discussion of the acts of the 1790's is based on the material in Prucha, *American Indian Policy in Its Formative Years,* pp. 45-49, 50, 62, 145, 215-17. Jefferson's act of March 1802 put on a more permanent basis the temporary acts of 1796 and 1799, *ibid.,* 50, 251.

9 For a discussion of the factory system see Ora K. Peake, *A History of the United States Indian Factory System, 1795-1822* (Denver, 1954).

10 Richardson, ed. *Messages and Papers of the Presidents*, I, 185.

11 Knox's report of December 29, 1794, is in *American State Papers, Indian Affairs*, I, 543-44.

Chapter 5: The South, 1789-1799

1 *American State Papers, Indian Affairs*, I, 12, 15-16.

2 *Ibid.*, 38.

3 *Ibid.*, 48-49.

4 *Ibid.*, 52-54.

5 *Ibid.*, 54-55.

6 *Ibid.*, 65-68.

7 The proceedings of the commissioners and their letter to Knox of November 20, 1789, are *ibid.*, 68-80. Knox's report of January 4, 1790, is *ibid.*, 59-61.

8 See Carter, *Territorial Papers*, IV, 3-19, 24. For Blount's attitude towards his appointment see Masterson, *Blount*, 174-79.

9 Cession of December 21, 1789, is in *American State Papers, Indian Affairs*, I, 114. For the Yazoo land companies of 1789 see Thomas P. Abernethy, *The South in the New Nation, 1789-1819* (Louisiana State Univ. Press, 1961), pp. 74 ff.

10 Willett's mission is discussed in Caughey, *McGillivray of the Creeks*, pp. 40-42; also McGillivray to William Panton, May 8, 1790, *ibid.*, pp. 259-62.

11 *Ibid.*, pp. 43-45 for discussion of McGillivray's visit to New York, and documents in *ibid.*, 273-79; also Cotterill, *Southern Indians*, 85-87. The treaty is in *Statutes at Large*, VII, 35-38, and drafts of the secret articles in the Henry Knox Papers, XXVI, 129-30; also see Henry Knox Papers, XXVI, 120, 122, 124, 128, 137, 145.

12 See Nathaniel Pendleton to Knox, November 1, 1790; Briggs to Benjamin Hawkins, December 16, 1790; Henry Knox Papers, XXVII, 43, 83.

13 *American State Papers, Indian Affairs*, I, 83.

14 Knox to Washington, March 10, 1791, Carter, *Territorial Papers*, IV, 50-52; Blount's role in signing the treaty is discussed in Masterson, *Blount*, pp. 196-207. Treaty of Holston is in Carter, *Territorial Papers*, IV, 60-67.

15 *American State Papers, Indian Affairs*, I, 135, 203-207. Land speculators had shown great interest in the Muscle Shoals region, and Blount had been directly involved. See Arthur P. Whitaker, "The Muscle Shoals Speculation, 1783-1789," *Mississippi Valley Historical Review*, XIII (1926), 365-86, and Charles H. Haskins "The Yazoo Land Companies," American Historical Association, *Papers*, V, Part 4 (1891), 414.

16 Carter, *Territorial Papers*, IV, 111-15, 120; *American State Papers, Indian Affairs*, I, 628-29.

Notes

[17] Carter, *Territorial Papers,* IV, 34.

[18] Knox to the Chickasaws, February 17, 1792, *American State Papers, Indian Affairs,* I, 249; Knox to Blount, January 31, February 16, 1792, Carter, *Territorial Papers,* IV, 115-19.

[19] There is considerable information on Creek and Cherokee hostility in *American State Papers, Indian Affairs,* I, 263 ff.; for population of Mero District in spring of 1794 see report of Knox to Washington, April 11, 1794, Carter, *Territorial Papers,* IV, 337.

[20] Knox to Blount, April 22, 1792, Carter, *Territorial Papers,* IV, 137-42; see also Blount, to James Robertson, April 1, 1792; Blount to Knox, May 5, 16, July 4, 1792; *ibid.,* IV, 132-36, 148-49, 150-52, 157-59.

[21] Knox to Washington, July 28, 1792; Knox to Blount, August 15, 1792; Blount to Knox, September 11, 1792; *ibid.,* IV, 159-68.

[22] Knox to Blount, June 26, 1793; Blount and Pickens to Knox, August 1, 1793; *ibid.,* IV, 278-79, 291-93; also Knox to Blount, August 26, 1793; Blount to Knox, October 18, 1793; *ibid.,* IV, 299-300, 308. There is considerable information on the Indian depredations of 1793 in *American State Papers, Indian Affairs,* I, 363 ff.

[23] See "Report of Committee of Congress: Territorial Defense," April 8, 1794; Report of Knox to the President, April 11, 1794; and "A Bill for the Protection of the Territory," May 29, 1794, Carter, *Territorial Papers,* IV, 335-38, 342-43.

[24] *Ibid.,* IV, 346-48; Cotterill, *Southern Indians,* pp. 110-11.

[25] See Blount to Knox, September 21, November 10, 28, 1794, Carter, *Territorial Papers,* IV, 354-55, 364-70, 373; *American State Papers, Indian Affairs,* I, 632-35.

[26] The Georgia Act of Appropriation, December 28, 1794 and Supplementary Act of January 7, 1795, are in *American State Papers, Indian Affairs,* I, 551-55. For the activities of the Yazoo companies see Charles H. Haskins, "The Yazoo Land Companies," American Historical Association, *Papers,* V, No. 4 (1891), 414-24, and Abernethy, *The South in the New Nation,* pp. 136-68.

[27] Knox to Blount, March 23, 1795, Carter, *Territorial Papers,* IV, 386-93.

[28] See Washington to Senate, June 25, 1795, and accompanying letters, *American State Papers, Indian Affairs,* I, 560-61. For the proceedings at the treaty and the clash with the Georgia commissioners see *ibid.,* I, 586-616. The treaty is in *Statutes at Large,* VII, 56-60.

[29] See Prucha, *American Indian Policy,* pp. 149-54, and Masterson, *Blount,* pp. 328-31.

[30] McHenry to Moore, Walton, and Steel, March 30, 1798, *American State Papers, Indian Affairs,* I, 639-40. The negotiations in the fall were carried on by Walton and a new appointee, Lieutenant Thomas Butler, *ibid.,* I, 640. The treaty is in *Statutes at Large,* VII, 62-65; see also Charles C. Royce, "The Cherokee Nation of Indians," *Fifth Annual Report of the Bureau of Ethnology* (Washington, 1887), pp. 174-83.

31 McHenry to Lewis, March 30, 1799, War Department, Secretary's Office, Letters Sent, Indian Affairs, A: 29-35, National Archives, Washington, D. C.

Chapter 6: The Old Northwest, 1789-1795

1 For the attacks on Kentucky and Kentucky's reaction see Gayle Thornbrough, ed. *Outpost on the Wabash, 1787-1791: Letters of Brigadier General Josiah Harmar and Major John Francis Hamtramck and Other Letters and Documents Selected from the Harmar Papers in the William L. Clements Library* (Indiana Historical Society Publications, Indianapolis, 1957), XIX, 166-71, 175-77, 182; also Carter, ed. *Territorial Papers*, II, 216-17.

2 *Annals of Congress*, 1 Congress, 1 Session, pp. 2199-2200; Washington to St. Clair, October 6, 1789, Smith, ed. *St. Clair Papers*, II, 125-26; Knox to St. Clair, December 19, 1789, Carter, ed. *Territorial Papers*, II, 224-26.

3 St. Clair's efforts of the winter of 1789-90 can be followed from the letters in Smith, ed. *St. Clair Papers*, II, 129-33, 135, and in Thornbrough, ed. *Outpost on the Wabash*, 222-25; St. Clair to Knox, May 1, 1790, Smith, ed. *St. Clair Papers*, II, 136-40; St. Clair to Washington, May 1, 1790, Carter, ed. *Territorial Papers*, II, 244-45.

4 See Smith, ed. *St. Clair Papers*, II, 146-48.

5 St. Clair to Knox, August 23, 1790, *American State Papers, Indian Affairs*, I, 92-93.

6 Knox to St. Clair, August 23, 1790, Smith, ed. *St. Clair Papers*, II, 162-63; Knox to St. Clair, September 12, 1790, *American State Papers, Indian Affairs*, I, 100.

7 See Hamtramck to Harmar, November 2, 1790, Thornbrough, ed. *Outpost on the Wabash*, 259-64.

8 See Harmar to the Secretary of War, November 4, 1790, *American State Papers, Indian Affairs*, I, 104; Harmar to Hamtramck, November 29, 1790, Thornbrough, ed. *Outpost on the Wabash*, 268-69; "Journal of Major Denny," *Memoirs of the Historical Society of Pennsylvania*, VII, 343-53; Information of Matthew Elliott, in *Michigan Pioneer and Historical Collections*, XXIV, 133-34.

9 *American State Papers, Indian Affairs*, I, 112-13.

10 *Statutes at Large*, I, 222-24; Denny to Harmar, March 9, 1791, Smith, ed. *St. Clair Papers*, II, 200-201.

11 See Knox to Procter, March 11, 1791, *American State Papers, Indian Affairs*, I, 145-46, and narrative of Procter, *ibid.*, I, 149-65; also Proceedings of a Council with the Six Nations, *Michigan Pioneer and Historical Collections*, XXV, 234-35.

12 For diversionary efforts of May and August see *American State Papers, Indian Affairs*, I, 129-35, and Smith, ed. *St. Clair Papers*, II, 212-16, 222-23, 227-29.

[13] The instructions to St. Clair are in *American State Papers, Indian Affairs*, I, 171-74.

[14] For St. Clair's defeat see James R. Jacobs, *The Beginning of the U. S. Army, 1783-1812* (Princeton, N. J., 1947), pp. 66-123.

[15] *American State Papers, Indian Affairs*, I, 197-99.

[16] Carter, ed. *Territorial Papers*, II, 359-66.

[17] Instructions to Pond and Steedman are in *American State Papers, Indian Affairs*, I, 227; see also *ibid.*, I, 235.

[18] See Octavius Pickering and Charles W. Upham, *The Life of Timothy Pickering* (4 vols., Boston, 1867-1873), III, 72-79; also *American State Papers, Indian Affairs*, I, 165-67.

[19] *American State Papers, Indian Affairs*, I, 226, 228-29; see also Katherine C. Turner, *Red Men Calling on the Great White Father* (Norman, Okla., 1951), pp. 10-11.

[20] *American State Papers, Indian Affairs*, I, 226, 228-31, 233, 236-37; also Stone, *Life of Brant*, II, 318-29.

[21] Knox to Trueman, April 3, 1792, *American State Papers, Indian Affairs*, I, 229-30; James Wilkinson to Hardin, May 20, 1792, *Michigan Pioneer and Historical Collections*, XXIV, 414-16; also see Buell, ed. *Memoirs of Putnam*, pp. 273-78, 301-304, 311-12, 313-16.

[22] The instructions to Putnam are in Buell, ed. *Memoirs of Putnam*, pp. 257-67.

[23] Putnam's travels to the West can be followed in Putnam to Knox, July 5, 8, 14, 22, August 16, 1792, *ibid.*, pp. 273-78, 280-90, 295-97, 301-304, 321-24. Knox to Putnam, August 7, 1792, is *ibid.*, pp. 313-16.

[24] The minutes of the treaty council are *ibid.*, pp. 335-62. The treaty is in *American State Papers, Indian Affairs*, I, 338.

[25] See *American State Papers, Indian Affairs*, I, 338; Buell, ed. *Memoirs of Putnam*, pp. 377-78; *Journal of the Executive Proceedings of the Senate of the United States of America* (Washington, 1828-   ), I, 128, 134-35, 144-46.

[26] The proceedings of the Indian council are in Ernest A. Cruikshank, ed. *The Correspondence of Lieut. Governor John Graves Simcoe* (5 vols., Toronto, 1923-1931), I, 218-29. See also Six Nations to the United States, November 16, 1792, *American State Papers, Indian Affairs*, I, 323-24; Stone, *Life of Brant*, II, 334; B. H. Coates, ed. "A Narrative of an Embassy to the Western Indians from the Original Manuscript of Hendrick Aupaumut," *Memoirs of the Historical Society of Pennsylvania*, II (Philadelphia, 1827), 115-22.

[27] Knox to the Western Indians, December 12, 1792, February 28, 1793, Cruikshank, ed. *Correspondence of Simcoe*, I, 270, 295; Knox to Wayne, January 5, 1793, Knopf, ed. *Anthony Wayne*, pp. 164-67.

[28] Fitzpatrick, ed. *Writings of Washington*, XXXII, 348-49; Carter, *Territorial Papers*, II, 440-41; H. A. Washington, ed. *The Writings of Thomas Jefferson* (9 vols., New York, 1854), IX, 136-38.

²⁹ The instructions are in *American State Papers, Indian Affairs*, I, 340-42.

³⁰ The western journey of the commissioners and their negotiations with the Indians can be followed in *American State Papers, Indian Affairs*, I, 342-60. Indian speech of July 30 is *ibid.*, I, 352, and reply of commissioners is *ibid.*, I, 352-54; the final Indian reply is *ibid.*, 356-57. See also Benjamin Lincoln, "Journal of a Treaty Held in 1793, with the Indian Tribes North-West of the Ohio, by Commissioners of the United States," *Collections of the Massachusetts Historical Society*, 3rd Series, V (Boston, 1836), 109-176, and "Expedition to Detroit," *Michigan Pioneer and Historical Collections*, XVII, 565-666.

³¹ Jefferson to Charles Pinckney, November 27, 1793, Washington, ed. *Writings of Jefferson*, IV, 85-86.

³² See Wayne to Knox, October 5, November 15, 1793, Knopf, ed. *Anthony Wayne*, pp. 275-77, 281-84. For the course of events leading up to Fallen Timbers and the battle itself see the correspondence *ibid.*, 339-61; also Jacobs, *Beginning of the U. S. Army*, pp. 124-88.

³³ The instructions to Knox on April 4, 1794, are in Northwest Territory Collection, William Henry Smith Library, Indianapolis. For the negotiations of the 1794-1795 winter see Wayne to the Indians, September 12, 1794, Cruikshank, ed. *Correspondence of Simcoe*, III, 79-80; *American State Papers, Indian Affairs*, I, 527-28, 559-60; Knopf, ed. *Anthony Wayne*, pp. 361-90, Cruikshank, ed. *Correspondence of Simcoe*, III, 252-53, 275-76, 279-80, 287-90, 290-91, 315-16.

³⁴ Pickering's letter of April 8, postscript of April 14, 1795, and letter of April 15 are in Knopf, ed. *Anthony Wayne*, pp. 393-407. The suggested treaty with the western Indians, April 1795, is in the Northwest Territory Collection, William Henry Smith Library, Indianapolis.

³⁵ Pickering to Rufus King, June 1, 1785, Charles R. King, ed. *The Life and Correspondence of Rufus King* (6 vols., New York, 1894-1900), I, 104-105.

³⁶ The minutes of the Greenville Treaty Council are in *American State Papers, Indian Affairs*, I, 564-82.

³⁷ The Treaty of Greenville is in *Statutes at Large*, VII, 49-54. For how Wayne obtained more than Pickering had suggested see Wayne to Pickering, May 15, September 2 and Pickering to Wayne, June 29, 1795, Knopf, ed. *Anthony Wayne*, pp. 415-19, 447-53, 430-34.

³⁸ See Carter, *Territorial Papers*, II, 22-24, 84-86; Treat, *National Land System*, pp. 319-25.

³⁹ Carter, *Territorial Papers*, II, 6-9, 18; Donaldson, *Public Domain*, pp. 233-34.

⁴⁰ See below pp. 149-51.

⁴¹ Carter, *Territorial Papers*, II, 567-68.

Notes

Chapter 7: The Ambivalence of Thomas Jefferson

[1] Carter, ed. *Territorial Papers,* III, 86-88.

[2] Jefferson to Chastellux, June 7, 1785; to Edward Carrington, January 16, 1787; Boyd, ed. *Jefferson Papers,* VIII, 185, XI, 49.

[3] Jefferson's Observations on Demeunier's Manuscript (completed June 22, 1786), *ibid.,* X, 44.

[4] Jefferson to Hawkins, August 13, 1786, *ibid.,* X, 240.

[5] Jefferson to the chiefs of the Wyandots, Ottawas, Chippewas, Potawatomis, and Shawnees, January 1809, War Department, Secretary's Office, Letters Sent, Indian Affairs, B: 412-13, National Archives, Washington, D.C.

[6] Dearborn to Silas Dinsmoor, May 8, 1802, *ibid., A,* 207-212.

[7] Richardson, ed. *Messages and Papers of the Presidents,* I, 380.

[8] War Department, Secretary's Office, Letters Sent, Indian Affairs, B, 395-96; also Jefferson to deputation of the Six Nations, February 12, 1803; to deputation of the Choctaws, January 1804; *ibid.,* A: 315, 413-15.

[9] Jefferson to Hawkins, February 18, 1803, Paul L. Ford, ed. *The Writings of Thomas Jefferson,* VIII, 213-15.

[10] Richardson, ed. *Messages and Papers of the Presidents,* I, 352-53.

[11] See Jefferson to Robert Livingston, April 18, 1802, Ford, ed. *Writings of Jefferson,* VIII, 145.

[12] Jefferson to Harrison, February 27, 1803, Logan Esarey, ed. *Messages and Letters of William Henry Harrison* (2 vols., Indianapolis, 1922), I, 69-73.

[13] Richardson, ed. *Messages and Papers of the Presidents,* I, 386-87, also *ibid.,* I, 326 (Annual Message of December 1801).

[14] *Ibid.,* I, 407, 454.

[15] Jefferson to Beaver, the head warrior of the Delawares, December 1808, War Department, Secretary's Office, Letters Sent, Indian Affairs, B: 406.

[16] For a discussion of Jefferson's ideas of Indian removal see Annie H. Abel, "The History of Events Resulting in Indian Consolidation West of the Mississippi," American Historical Association, *Annual Report, 1906* (Washington, 1908), I, 241-59.

[17] Dearborn to Chouteau, July 17, 1804, War Department, Secretary's Office, Letters Sent, Indian Affairs, B: 10-11. For Jefferson's speeches to Indians from the trans-Mississippi West see *ibid.,* B: 13-15, 145-46, 200-203, 204, 266-69, 269-73.

Chapter 8: The South, 1799-1809

[1] Pickering to Sargent, May 20, 1799, Carter, ed. *Territorial Papers,* V, 56-60.

2 Hawkins to Jefferson, June 14, 1786, Boyd, ed. *Jefferson Papers*, IX, 641.

3 Dexter to Hawkins, December 9, 1800, War Department, Secretary's Office, Letters Sent, Indian Affairs, A:5.

4 *Ibid.*, A:44.

5 See Dearborn to Wilkinson, to John McKee, to Return J Meigs, and to the Cherokees, Chickasaws, and Choctaws, June 18, 1801, *ibid.*, A: 53, 54-55, 55-56.

6 Instructions re the Cherokees are in War Department, Secretary's Office, Letters Sent, Indian Affairs, A: 59-63.

7 See minutes of meetings of Cherokees and Dearborn at the War Office, June 30, July 3, 1801, *ibid.*, A: 72-83.

8 *Ibid.*, A: 83-85, 87-89.

9 Instructions re Chickasaws and Choctaws are in *ibid.*, A: 63-67.

10 *Ibid.*, A: 103-105.

11 See *American State Papers, Indian Affairs*, I, 656-57. Also Hawkins to Dearborn, September 6, 1801, War Department, Secretary's Office, Letters Received, Indian Affairs, Roll I, 1800-1816, pp. 26-28, National Archives, Washington, D.C.

12 See Wilkinson, Hawkins, and Pickens to Dearborn, October 25, 1801, *ibid.*, I, 651-52. The Treaty of Chickasaw Bluffs is in *Statutes at Large*, VII, 65-66. See also Cotterill, *Southern Indians*, pp. 133-34.

13 The minutes of the Fort Adams Treaty Conference are in *American State Papers, Indian Affairs*, I, 660-63. The treaty is in *Statutes at Large*, VII, 66-68; also Wilkinson, Hawkins, and Pickens to Dearborn, December 18, 1801, War Department, Secretary's Office, Letters Received, Indian Affairs, Roll I, 1800-1816, pp. 162-66.

14 Dearborn to the commissioners, April 12, 1802, War Department, Secretary's Office, Letters Sent, Indian Affairs, A: 199.

15 *Ibid.*, A: 200-202.

16 Georgia act of cession is in Carter, ed. *Territorial Papers*, V, 142-46.

17 For the proceedings with the Creeks see *American State Papers, Indian Affairs*, I, 668-81. See also Dearborn to Wilkinson and Hawkins, June 10, 1802, War Department, Secretary's Office, Letters Sent, Indian Affairs, A: 225, and *ibid.*, A: 238-39; Wilkinson, Hawkins, and Pickens to Dearborn, June 17, 1802, War Department, Secretary's Office, Letters Received, Indian Affairs, Roll I, 1800-1816, pp. 122-24. The Fort Wilkinson Treaty is in *Statutes at Large*, VII, 68-70.

18 Wilkinson and Hawkins to Dearborn, July 15, 1802, *American State Papers, Indian Affairs*, I, 669-70.

19 See Dearborn to Wilkinson, June 2, 1802, War Department, Secretary's Office, Letters Sent, Indian Affairs, A: 218-19. Wilkinson to Dearborn, August 20, 1803, War Department, Secretary's Office, Letters Received, Indian Affairs, Roll I, 1800-1816, pp. 205-

212. For treaties at Fort Confederation and Hoe Buckintoopa see *Statutes at Large,* VII, 73-74, 80.

20 Dearborn to Meigs, February 19, 1803, War Department, Secretary's Office, Letters Sent, Indian Affairs, A: 323-24. A conference was held with the Cherokee chiefs on April 20-23; the proceedings are in Records of the Cherokee Indian Agency in Tennessee, 1801-1835, Correspondence and Misc. Records, 1803-1804. Also see *ibid.,* Meigs to Dearborn, May 4, 1803.

21 Dearborn to Meigs, May 30, 1803, War Department, Secretary's Office, Letters Sent, Indian Affairs, A: 352-53; Dearborn to Joseph Anderson, November 21, 1803, to John Milledge, November 21, 1803, *ibid.,* A: 388-92. For Cherokee agreement to the road see Meigs to Dearborn, October 25, 1803, Records of the Cherokee Indian Agency in Tennessee, 1801-1835, Correspondence and Misc. Records, 1803-1804.

22 Dearborn to Meigs and Smith, April 4, 1804, War Department, Secretary's Office, Letters Sent, Indian Affairs, A: 459-60.

23 Dearborn to Meigs, April 23, 1804, to Hooker, April 23, 1804, *ibid.,* B: 1-2.

24 The Treaty of Tellico (October 24, 1804) is in *Statutes at Large,* VII, 228; see also Royce, "Cherokee Nation of Indians," *Fifth Annual Report of the Bureau of Ethnology,* 183-88. There was a long delay in the ratification of the Treaty of Tellico owing to a disagreement over the boundaries of the ceded tract, see Meigs to William Eustis, December 20, 1811, War Department, Secretary's Office, Letters Received, Indian Affairs, Roll I, 1800-1816, pp. 727-29.

25 For failure in the early summer see Meigs and Daniel Smith to Dearborn, July 27, 1805, Records of the Cherokee Indian Agency in Tennessee, 1801-1835, Correspondence and Misc. Records, 1805-1807; Dearborn to Meigs, October 8, 1805, War Department, Secretary's Office, Letters Sent, Indian Affairs, B: 117.

26 The Treaties of Tellico (October 25 and 27, 1805) are in *Statutes at Large,* VII, 93-96. See also Meigs to Dearborn, September 22, 1805, Records of the Cherokee Agency in Tennessee, 1801-1835, Correspondence and Misc. Records, 1805-1807; Royce, "Cherokee Nation of Indians," *Fifth Annual Report of the Bureau of Ethnology,* pp. 189-93.

27 Jefferson's talk of January 10, 1806, to the chiefs of the Cherokee nation is in War Department, Secretary's Office, Letters Sent, Indian Affairs, B: 147-48. The convention signed at Washington (January 7, 1806) is in *Statutes at Large,* VII, 101-103.

28 War Department, Secretary's Office Letters Sent, Indian Affairs, B: 153.

29 Dearborn to Hawkins, February 19, 1803, *ibid.,* A: 325-26.

30 Dearborn to Wilkinson, Hawkins, and Robert Anderson, May 5, 1803, *ibid.,* A: 342-44, and *ibid.,* 344-45; also Dearborn to Hawkins, May 24, 1803, *ibid.,* A: 349-51.

31 See Dearborn to Thomas Freeman, to Hawkins, to Governor John Milledge of Georgia, October 6, 1803, *ibid.*, A: 380-83.

32 Dearborn to Hawkins, to Merriwether, to Milledge, April 2, 1804, to Hawkins, November 22, 1803, February 11, 1804, *ibid.*, A: 456-59, 395, 435-36. The Treaty of November 3, 1804, is in *American State Papers, Indian Affairs*, I, 691, and Jefferson's message submitting it to the Senate (December 14, 1804), *ibid.*, I, 690-91.

33 Dearborn to Hawkins, February 12, 1805, War Department, Secretary's Office, Letters Sent, Indian Affairs, B: 41-42.

34 Jefferson's talk of November 2, 1805, to the Creeks chiefs is *ibid.*, B: 154-56. See also Dearborn to Hawkins, June 28, 1805, *ibid.*, B: 88.

35 *Ibid.*, B: 157-60.

36 The Washington Treaty of November 14, 1805, is in *Statutes at Large*, VII, 96-98.

37 See Jefferson to the Senate, January 7, 1803, *American State Papers, Indian Affairs*, I, 681.

38 Dearborn to Wilkinson, February 21, 1803, War Department, Secretary's Office, Letters Sent, Indian Affairs, A: 326-27. See also Wilkinson to Silas Dinsmoor, August 19, 1803, to Dearborn, October 1, 1803, War Department, Secretary's Office, Letters Received, Indian Affairs, Roll I, 1800-1816, pp. 219-25, 241-48.

39 *Ibid.*, A: 408-409, 412-17; also Dearborn to General Irvine, December 19, 1803, *ibid.*, A: 405-406.

40 Ephraim Kirby to Jefferson, April 20, 1804, Carter, ed. *Territorial Papers*, V, 317-19.

41 Dearborn to Dinsmoor, October 25, 1804, War Department, Secretary's Office, Letters Sent, Indian Affairs, B: 19-21.

42 Dearborn to Robertson and Dinsmoor, March 20, 1805, *ibid.*, B: 47-52.

43 Dearborn to Robertson, August 27, 1805, to Dinsmoor, August 28, 29, 1805, *ibid.*, B: 100-103: Cotterill, *Southern Indians*, p. 147.

44 The Treaty of July 23, 1805, is in *Statutes at Large*, VII, 89-90; also Dearborn to Robertson, July 3, 1805, War Department, Secretary's Office, Letters Sent, Indian Affairs, B: 88.

45 See Cotterill, *Southern Indians*, 149. The Treaty of November 16 is in *Statutes at Large*, VII, 98-100. See also Jefferson to the Senate, January 15, 1808, *American State Papers, Indian Affairs*, I, 748-49.

46 Dearborn to Robertson, May 15, 1806, Dearborn to Wright, March 26, 1807, War Department, Secretary's Office, Letters Sent, Indian Affairs, B: 222, 297.

47 Dearborn to Hawkins, September 10, 1806, *ibid.*, B: 253-54.

48 Dearborn to Meigs, Robertson, April 1, 1807, *ibid.*, B: 299-302.

49 Dearborn to Wright, April 1, 1807, *ibid.*, B: 298-99; Dearborn to Colbert, April 17, 1807, *ibid.*, B: 307.

50 See Meigs to Dearborn, May 1, September 28, 1807, Records of the Cherokee Indian Agency in Tennessee, 1801 to 1835, Cor-

respondence and Misc. Records, 1805-1807. Doublehead was killed before he could take part in the running of the line, but other chiefs proved acquiescent.

[51] Dearborn to Meigs, March 25, May 5, 1808, Jefferson to chiefs of the Upper Cherokees, May 1, 1808, to deputies of the Cherokees of the Upper and Lower Towns, January 9, 1809, War Department, Secretary's Office, Letters Sent, Indian Affairs, B: 364, 374-75, 376-77, 414-17.

[52] Dearborn to Hawkins, May 8, December 12, 1808, *ibid.*, 377-78, 408.

[53] Thomas Freeman to Albert Gallatin, March 4, 1809, Carter, ed. *Territorial Papers*, V, 720-22.

Chapter 9: The Old Northwest, 1795-1809

[1] Dearborn to Lyman, July 14, 1801, War Department, Secretary's Office, Letters Sent, Indian Affairs, A: 91-97.

[2] *Ibid.*, A: 135-43.

[3] *Ibid.*, A: 146.

[4] *Ibid.*, A: 233-38.

[5] For conference of September 1802 see Esarey, ed. *Messages and Letters of Harrison*, I, 56-57. See also Dorothy Burne Goebel, *William Henry Harrison: A Political Biography* (Indianapolis, 1926), pp. 98-101; Dearborn to Harrison, February 21, 1803, War Department, Secretary's Office, Letters Sent, Indian Affairs, A: 328-30.

[6] *Ibid.*, A: 329-30.

[7] Jefferson to Harrison, February 27, 1803, Esarey, ed. *Messages and Letters of Harrison*, I, 69-73.

[8] *Statutes at Large*, VII, 74-76 (June 7, 1803), 77 (August 7, 1803), also Goebel, *Harrison*, pp. 103-105.

[9] *Statutes at Large*, VII, 78-79; Richardson, ed. *Messages and Papers of the Presidents*, I, 359.

[10] Dearborn to Harrison, June 27, 1804, War Department, Secretary's Office, Letters Sent, Indian Affairs, B: 7-8.

[11] *Statutes at Large*, VII, 81-83 (August 18, 1804), 83-84 (August 27, 1804).

[12] *Ibid.*, VII, 84-87 (November 3, 1804).

[13] Richardson, ed. *Messages and Papers of the Presidents*, I, 372; Dearborn to William Wells, December 24, 1804, War Department, Secretary's Office, Letters Sent, Indian Affairs, B: 35-36; also Harrison to Dearborn, March 3, 1805, Esarey, ed. *Messages and Letters of Harrison*, I, 76-84. This letter is misdated by Esarey.

[14] Dearborn to Jouett, April 2, 1805, *ibid.*, B: 62-64.

[15] Dearborn to Harrison, June 11, 1805, *ibid.*, B: 84-85.

[16] The Treaty of Fort Industry is in *Statutes at Large*, VII, 87-89.

[17] The Treaty of Grouseland (August 21, 1805) is in *Statutes*

at Large, VII, 91-93. See also Harrison to Dearborn, August 10, 26, September 16, 1805, Esarey, ed. Messages and Letters of Harrison, I, 161-67.

18 Dearborn to Harrison, October 11, 1805, War Department, Secretary's Office, Letters Sent, Indian Affairs, B: 119-20. The Treaty of Vincennes (December 30, 1805) is in Statutes at Large, VII, 100-101; see also Harrison to Dearborn, January 1, 1806, Esarey, ed. Messages and Letters of Harrison, I, 184-85.

19 Jefferson to chiefs of the Fox, Sacs, and Potawatomis, January 1806, War Department, Secretary's Office, Letters Sent, Indian Affairs, B: 143-44; for encouragement given to Indians of Indiana see Dearborn to William Wells, February 28, 1806, ibid., B: 177, and Joseph A. Parsons, Jr., "Civilizing the Indians of the Old Northwest, 1800-1810," Indiana Magazine of History, LVI (1960), 195-216. Dearborn to Boilvin, April 10, 1806, War Department, Secretary's Office, Letters Sent, Indian Affairs, B: 195-96.

20 The most recent biography of Tecumseh is Glenn Tucker, Tecumseh: Vision of Glory (Indianapolis, 1956). Though detailed and colorful, the use of material is injudicious. Still useful for the origins of the conspiracy is James Mooney, "The Ghost-Dance Religion and the Sioux Outbreak of 1893," Fourteenth Annual Report of the Bureau of Ethnology, 1892-93 (Washington, 1896), pp. 670-91. Dearborn to Harrison, July 19, 1806, War Department, Secretary's Office, Letters Sent, Indian Affairs, B: 240.

21 Dearborn to Hull, July 22, 1806, ibid., B: 241-43.

22 Dearborn to Hull, November 22, 1806, January 27, 1807, ibid., B: 263, 275. The Treaty of Detroit (November 17, 1807) is in Statutes at Large, VII, 105-107.

23 Jefferson to the Shawnees, February 19, 1807, War Department, Secretary's Office, Letters Sent, Indian Affairs, B: 279-82.

24 The activities of the British agents are discussed in Reginald Horsman, Matthew Elliott: British Indian Agent (Detroit, 1964).

25 The Treaty of Brownstown (November 25, 1808) is in Statutes at Large, VII, 112-13.

26 War Department, Secretary's Office, Letters Sent, Indian Affairs, B: 369-73.

27 Ibid., B: 400-402, 405-408.

28 Dearborn to Kirk, December 22, 1808, to Captain Hendrick, December 27, 1808, ibid., 409-410.

Chapter 10: The Coming of War

1 Richardson, ed. Messages and Papers of the Presidents, I, 468.

2 Ibid., 475, 484 (December 5, 1810).

3 Smith to Meigs, March 13, 20, 1809, War Department, Secre-

tary's Office, Letters Sent, Indian Affairs, B: 432; Meigs to Smith, June 12, 1809, Carter, ed. *Territorial Papers*, V, 739-41.

[4] Eustis to Neely, November 17, 1809, to Hawkins, November 6, 1809; Madison to the Speaker of the Creek National Council, November 1809; War Department, Secretary's Office, Letters Sent, Indian Affairs, C: 9, 7-8.

[5] Governor David Holmes to Eustis, February 7, 1810, Carter, ed. *Territorial Papers*, VI, 44-45.

[6] Eustis to Neely, June 7, 1810, December 11, 1811, War Department, Secretary's Office, Letters Sent, Indian Affairs, C: 30, 105. See also Prucha, *American Indian Policy*, pp. 159-63.

[7] Eustis to Meigs, Hawkins, Dinsmoor, March 6, 1810, War Department, Secretary's Office, Letters Sent, Indian Affairs, C: 18.

[8] Eustis to Hawkins, January 15, 1811, to William Blount, February 12, 1811; Madison to the chiefs of the Creek Nation, January 14, 1811, *ibid.*, C: 58, 62, 57; Creeks to Madison, May 15, 1811, War Department, Secretary's Office, Letters Received, Indian Affairs, 1800-1823, Roll I, pp. 554-57.

[9] Eustis to Neely, March 11, May 25, 1811, *ibid.*, C: 66-67, 82.

[10] See Eustis to Blount, March 28, 1811, to Governor H. Middleton, March 28, 1811, *ibid.*, C: 70-71.

[11] See Eustis to Meigs, November 1, 1809, March 27, 1811, *ibid.*, C: 6, 69-70, and Eustis to Dinsmoor, April 20, 1811, *ibid.*, C: 77-78. Also Eustis to Meigs, May 25, 1811, *ibid.*, C: 83.

[12] Eustis to Neely, March 29, 1811, *ibid.*, C: 72.

[13] Eustis to Hawkins, June 27, 1811, War Department, Secretary's Office, Letters Sent, Indian Affairs, C: 85-86.

[14] Eustis to Hawkins, July 20, 1811, Eustis to Neely, August 17, 1811, *ibid.*, C: 90-92.

[15] Eustis to Harrison, July 15, 1809, *ibid.*, C: 2-3.

[16] These treaties are in *Statutes at Large*, VII, 115-17; see also Harrison to Eustis, October 1, November 3, December 10, 1809, Esarey, ed. *Messages and Letters of Harrison*, I, 358-59, 387-91, 396-97. The proceedings of the Treaties of Fort Wayne and of Vincennes (with the Weas) are *ibid.*, I, 362-78.

[17] For Harrison's fears of British activities among the Indians see Esarey, *Messages and Letters of Harrison*, I, *passim*.

[18] Eustis to Harrison, May 10, October 26, 1810, War Department, Secretary's Office, Letters Sent, Indian Affairs, C: 25, 52; Harrison to Eustis, April 25, 1810, Esarey, ed. *Messages and Letters of Harrison*, I, 417-19.

[19] Harrison to Eustis, December 24, 1810, Esarey, ed. *Messages and Letters of Harrison*, I, 496-500; Eustis to Harrison, March 7, 1811, War Department, Secretary's Office, Letters Sent, Indian Affairs, C: 66.

[20] Eustis to Harrison, July 17, 1811, to Governor Ninian Edwards, July 18, 1811, *ibid.*, C: 88-89. For the difficulties of 1811

see Esarey, ed. *Messages and Letters of Harrison,* I, pp. 532-50.

[21] Eustis to Harrison, July 20, September 18, 1811, War Department, Secretary's Office, Letters Sent, Indian Affairs, C: 90, 112-13.

[22] Eustis to Harrison, December 11, 25, 1811, *ibid.,* C: 104, 106. For the Battle of Tippecanoe see Alfred Pirtle, *The Battle of Tippecanoe* (Louisville, 1900); also Harrison to Eustis, November 8, 18, 1811, Esarey, ed. *Messages and Letters of Harrison,* I, 614-15, 618-31, also *ibid.,* I, 608-14, 616-18.

Bibliography

PRIMARY SOURCES

Manuscripts

The bulk of the manuscript material used for this book is in the National Archives, Washington, D.C., and much of it is now available on microfilm. Indispensable for an understanding of the 1780's are the Papers of the Continental Congress, 1774-1789. Of particular interest are Items 150 and 151, Letters from Major General Henry Knox, Secretary at War, 1785-1788, and Reports of Major General Henry Knox, 1785-1788. Also of importance are Item 153, Letters from Major General Philip Schuyler, 1775-1785; Item 30, Reports of Committee on Indian Affairs and Lands in the Western Territory, 1776-1789. Federal Indian records for the government under the Constitution mostly begin in 1800, owing to the fire which destroyed the 1790's material. Essential for this study were materials in Record Group 75, Records of the Bureau of Indian Affairs. In this period before 1812 Indian Affairs was under the control of the War Department, but much of the material has been separated from general War Department correspondence. Basic materials are in Letters Sent by the Secretary of War, Indian Affairs, 1800-1824, and in Letters Received by the Office of the Secretary of War relative to Indian Affairs, 1800-1823; also of value are Letters Sent by the Superintendent of Indian Trade, 1807-1823, and Records of the Cherokee Indian Agency in Tennessee, 1801-1835. There is also considerable material dealing with Indian affairs in Record Group 107, Records of the Office of the Secretary of War. Of most importance are Letters Sent, Military Affairs, 1800-1861, and Letters Received by the Secretary of War, Registered Series, 1803-1860. There is also material relating to Indian affairs in a number of other record groups, particularly in Record Group 46, Records of the United States Senate, Territorial Papers, 1789-1873.

There are of course a variety of collections outside of the National Archives which throw light on federal Indian policy in these years. Perhaps the most significant is the material in the Massachusetts Historical Society in Boston; the essential collections are the Henry Knox and the Timothy Pickering Papers. There is also a considerable amount of material in the Draper Manuscripts in the State Historical Society in Madison, Wisconsin, and I made use of material from the Wayne Manuscripts in the Historical Society of Pennsylvania in Philadelphia and the Northwest Territory Collection in the William Henry Smith Library of the Indiana Historical Society in Indianapolis.

Printed

There is a mass of printed source material which helps in the understanding of federal Indian policy in these years. The following is a list of the works that were most useful for this study.

American State Papers. Class II, Indian Affairs, I. Washington, 1832.
American State Papers. Class V, Military Affairs, I. Washington, 1832.
American State Papers. Public Lands, I. Washington, 1834.
Annals of the Congress of the United States. 42 vols. Washington, 1834-1856.
Boyd, Julian P., ed. *The Papers of Thomas Jefferson.* Princeton, 1950- .
Buell, Rowena, ed. *Memoirs of Rufus Putnam and Certain Official Papers and Correspondence.* Boston, 1903.
Burnett, Edmund C. *Letters of Members of the Continental Congress.* 8 vols. Washington, 1921-36.
Burton, Clarence M., ed., "Ephraim Douglass and His Times," in *Magazine of History with Notes and Queries,* extra numbers, III, 10, New York, 1910.
Butterfield, Consul W., ed. *Journal of Capt. Jonathan Heart . . . to Which Is Added the Dickinson-Harmar Correspondence of 1784-1785.* Albany, 1885.
———. *Washington-Irvine Correspondence.* Madison, Wis., 1882.
Carter, Clarence E., ed. *The Territorial Papers of the United States.* Washington, 1934- .
Coates, B. H., ed., "A Narrative of an Embassy to the Western Indians from the Original Manuscript of Hendrick Aupaumut,"

Bibliography

Memoirs of the Historical Society of Pennsylvania, II (Philadelphia, 1827), 61-133.

Craig, Neville B., ed. *The Olden Time.* 2 vols. Pittsburgh, 1848; reprinted Cincinnati, 1876.

Cruikshank, Ernest A., ed. *The Correspondence of Lieut. Governor John Graves Simcoe.* 5 vols. Toronto, 1923-31.

Denny, Ebeneezer, "Military Journal of Major Ebeneezer Denny," *Memoirs of the Historical Society of Pennsylvania,* VII (Philadelphia, 1860), 237-409.

Esarey, Logan, ed. *Messages and Letters of William Henry Harrison.* 2 vols. Indianapolis, 1922.

Fitzpatrick, John C., ed. *The Writings of George Washington from the Original Manuscript Sources, 1745-1799,* 39 vols. Washington, 1931-44.

Ford, Paul L. *The Writings of Thomas Jefferson.* 10 vols. New York, 1892-99.

Ford, Worthington C., *et. al.,* eds. *Journals of the Continental Congress, 1774-1789.* 34 vols. Washington, 1904-37.

Hamer, P. M., ed., "Letters of Governor William Blount," East Tennessee Historical Society, *Publications,* IV (1932), 122-37.

Hastings, Hugh, ed. *The Public Papers of George Clinton.* 10 vols. New York, 1899-1914.

Hawkins, Benjamin. *Letters of Benjamin Hawkins, 1796-1806.* Collections of the Georgia Historical Society, IX. Savannah, 1916.

King, Charles R., ed. *The Life and Correspondence of Rufus King.* 6 vols. New York 1894-1900.

Knopf, Richard C., ed. *Anthony Wayne: A Name in Arms: Soldier, Diplomat, Defender of Expansion Westward of a Nation: The Wayne-Knox-Pickering-McHenry Correspondence.* Pittsburgh, 1960.

Lincoln, Benjamin, "Journal of a Treaty Held in 1793, with the Indian Tribes North-West of the Ohio, by Commissioners of the United States," *Collections of the Massachusetts Historical Society,* Third Series, V (Boston, 1836), 109-76.

Maclay, Edgar S. *The Journal of William Maclay, United States Senator from Pennsylvania, 1789-1791.* New York, 1929.

Michigan Pioneer and Historical Collections. 40 vols. Lansing, Michigan, 1877-1929.

Miller, Hunter, ed. *Treaties and Other International Acts of the United States of America 1776-1863.* 8 vols. Washington, 1931-1948.

Richardson, James D., comp. *A Compilation of the Messages and Papers of the Presidents.* 10 vols. Washington, 1896-99.

Rowland, Dunbar, ed. *The Mississippi Territorial Archives, 1798-1803.* Nashville, 1905.

Smith, William H., ed. *The Life and Public Services of Arthur St. Clair, Soldier of the Revolutionary War; President of the Continental Congress; and Governor of the North-Western Territory, with His Correspondence and Other Papers.* 2 vols. Cincinnati, 1882.

Statutes at Large of the United States of America. VII. Boston, 1853.

Storm, Colton, ed. "Up the Tennessee in 1790: The Report of Major John Doughty to the Secretary of War," East Tennessee Historical Society, *Publications*, XVII (1945), pp. 119-32.

Thornbrough, Gayle. *Outpost on the Wabash, 1787-1791: Letters of Brigadier General Josiah Harmar and Major John Francis Hamtramck and Other Letters and Documents Selected from the Harmar Papers in the William L. Clements Library.* Indianapolis, 1957.

Washington, H. A., ed. *The Writings of Thomas Jefferson.* 9 vols. New York, 1854.

White, Robert H. *Messages of the Governors of Tennessee.* 5 vols. Nashville, 1952-59.

SECONDARY SOURCES

Books

Abernethy, Thomas P. *From Frontier to Plantation in Tennessee; a Study in Frontier Democracy.* Chapel Hill, 1932.

——. *Western Lands and the American Revolution.* New York, 1937.

——. *The South in the New Nation, 1789-1819.* Baton Rouge, 1961.

Bond, Beverley W., Jr. *The Civilization of the Old Northwest; a Study of Political, Social, and Economic Development, 1788-1812.* New York, 1934.

Burt, A. L. *The United States, Great Britain and British North America, from the Revolution to the Establishment of Peace after the War of 1812.* New Haven, 1940.

Caughey, John W. *McGillivray of the Creeks.* Norman, Okla., 1938.

Cotterill, R. S. *The Southern Indians: The Story of the Civilized Tribes before Removal.* Norman, Okla., 1954.

Cushman, H. B. *History of the Choctaw, Chickasaw and Natchez Indians.* Greenville, Texas, 1899.

Dawson, Moses. *A Historical Narrative of the Civil and Military Services of Major-General William Henry Harrison.* Cincinnati, 1824.

Donaldson, Thomas. *The Public Domain.* Washington, 1884.

Downes, Randolph C. *Council Fires on the Upper Ohio: A Narrative of Indian Affairs in the Upper Ohio Valley until 1795.* Pittsburgh, 1940.

——. *Frontier Ohio, 1788-1803.* Columbus, Ohio, 1935.

Fenton, William N. *American Indian and White Relations to 1830: Needs and Opportunities for Study.* Chapel Hill, 1957.

Ferguson, E. James. *The Power of the Purse: A History of American Public Finance, 1776-1790.* Chapel Hill, 1961.

Goebel, Dorothy B. *William Henry Harrison: A Political Biography.* Indianapolis, 1926.

Bibliography

Harmon, George D. *Sixty Years of Indian Affairs: Political, Economic, and Diplomatic, 1789-1850.* Chapel Hill, 1941.

Hibbard, Benjamin H. *A History of the Public Land Policies.* New York, 1924.

Hodge, Frederick, W., ed. *Handbook of American Indians North of Mexico.* 2 vols. United States Bureau of Ethnology, Bulletin 30, Washington, 1912.

Kappler, Charles J. *Indian Affairs, Laws and Treaties.* 3 vols. Washington, 1904-1913.

Malone, Henry T. *Cherokees of the Old South: A People in Transition.* Athens, Georgia, 1956.

McLendon, S. G. *History of the Public Domain of Georgia.* Atlanta, 1924.

McReynolds, Edwin C. *The Seminoles.* Norman, Okla., 1957.

Manley, Henry S. *The Treaty of Fort Stanwix, 1784.* Rome, N. Y., 1932.

Masterson, William H. *William Blount.* Baton Rouge, 1954.

Mohr, Walter H. *Federal Indian Relations, 1774-1788.* Philadelphia, 1933.

Parker, Thomas V. *The Cherokee Indians, with Special Reference to their Relations with the United States Government.* New York, 1907.

Peake, Ora Brooks. *A History of the United States Indian Factory System, 1795-1822.* Denver, 1954.

Pearce, Roy Harvey. *The Savages of America. A Study of the Indian and the Idea of Civilization.* Baltimore, 1953.

Pickering, Octavius and Charles W. Upham. *The Life of Timothy Pickering.* 4 vols. Boston, 1867-73.

Pound, Merritt B. *Benjamin Hawkins: Indian Agent.* Athens, Georgia, 1951.

Prucha, Francis Paul. *American Indian Policy in the Formative Years: The Indian Trade and Intercourse Acts, 1790-1834.* Cambridge, Mass., 1962.

Royce, Charles C., comp. *Indian Land Cessions in the United States.* Eighteenth Annual Report of the Bureau of American Ethnology, 1896-97, Part II. Washington, 1899.

Stone, William L. *Life of Joseph Brant.* 2 vols. New York, 1838.

Treat, Payson J. *The National Land System, 1785-1820.* New York, 1910.

Tucker, Glenn. *Tecumseh: Vision of Glory.* Indianapolis, 1956.

Turner, Katherine C. *Red Men Calling on the Great White Father.* Norman, Okla., 1951.

Weinberg, Albert K. *Manifest Destiny: A Study of Nationalist Expansionism in American History.* Baltimore, 1935.

Williams, Samuel C. *Beginnings of West Tennessee in the Land of the Chickasaws, 1541-1841.* Johnson City, Tennessee, 1930.

———. *History of the Lost State of Franklin.* New York, 1933.

Whitaker, Arthur P. *The Mississippi Question: A Study in Trade, Politics, and Diplomacy.* New York, 1934.

——. *The Spanish-American Frontier, 1783-1795: The Westward Movement and the Spanish Retreat in the Mississippi Valley.* Boston, 1927.
Woodward, Grace Steele. *The Cherokees.* Norman, Okla., 1963.

Articles

Abel, Annie H., "The History of Events Resulting in Indian Consolidation West of the Mississippi," *Annual Report of the American Historical Association for the Year 1906* (Washington, 1908), pp. 233-450.
——, "Proposals for an Indian State, 1778-1878," *Annual Report of the American Historical Association for 1907* (Washington, 1908), I, 87-104.
Berry, Jane M., "The Indian Policy of Spain in the Southwest, 1783-1795," *Mississippi Valley Historical Review*, III (1917), 462-77.
Cotterill, R. S., "A Chapter of Panton, Leslie and Company," *Journal of Southern History*, X (1944), 274-92.
——, "Federal Indian Management in the South, 1789-1825," *Mississippi Valley Historical Review*, XX (1933), 333-52.
——, "The Virginia-Chickasaw Treaty of 1783," *Journal of Southern History*, VII (1941), 483-96.
Downes, Randolph C. "Cherokee-American Relations in the Upper Tennessee Valley, 1776-1791," *East Tennessee Historical Society, Publications*, VIII (1936), 35-53.
——, "Creek-American Relations, 1782-1790," *Georgia Historical Quarterly*, XXI (1937), 142-84.
——, "Creek-American Relations, 1790-1795," *Journal of Southern History*, VIII (1942), 350-73.
Hamer, Philip P., "The British in Canada and the Southern Indians, 1790-1794," *East Tennessee Historical Society, Publications*, II (1930), 107-34.
Haskins, Charles H., "The Yazoo Land Companies," *Papers of the American Historical Association*, V (1891), 395-437.
Horsman, Reginald, "American Indian Policy in the Old Northwest, 1783-1812," *William and Mary Quarterly*, XVIII (1961), 35-53.
——, "The British Indian Department and the Abortive Treaty of Lower Sandusky, 1793," *Ohio Historical Quarterly*, LXX (1961), 189-213.
——, "The British Indian Department and the Resistance to General Anthony Wayne, 1793-1795," *Mississippi Valley Historical Review*, XLIX (1962), 269-90.
——, "British Indian Policy in the Northwest, 1807-1812," *Mississippi Valley Historical Review*, XLV (1958), 51-66.
Leavitt, O. E., "British Policy on the Canadian Frontier, 1782-1792: Mediation and an Indian Barrier State," *Wisconsin Historical*

Society, *Proceedings* (1915), pp. 151-85.

McMurry, Donald L., "The Indian Policy of the Federal Government and the Economic Development of the Southwest, 1789-1801," *Tennessee Historical Magazine*, I (1915), 21-39, 106-119.

Mooney, James, "The Ghost Dance Religion and the Sioux Outbreak of 1893, *Fourteenth Annual Report of the Bureau of Ethnology, 1892-93* (Washington, 1896), pp. 670-91.

Parsons, Joseph A., Jr., "Civilizing the Indians of the Old Northwest," *Indiana Magazine of History*, LVI (1960), 195-216.

Royce, Charles C., "The Cherokee Nation of Indians: A Narrative of Their Official Relations with the Colonial and Federal Governments," *Fifth Annual Report of the Bureau of Ethnology, 1883-84* (Washington, 1887), 121-378.

Smith, Dwight L., "Wayne and the Treaty of Green Ville," *Ohio Archeological and Historical Quarterly*, LXIII (1954), 1-7.

Washburn, Wilcomb E., "A Moral History of Indian-White Relations: Needs and Opportunities for Study," *Ethnohistory*, IV (1957), 47-61.

———, "The Moral and Legal Justifications for Dispossessing the Indians," in James Morton Smith, ed., *Seventeenth-Century America: Essays in Colonial History*. Chapel Hill, 1959.

Whitaker, Arthur P., "Alexander McGillivray, 1783-1793," *North Carolina Historical Review*, V (1928), 181-203, 289-309.

———, "The Muscle Shoals Speculation, 1783-1789," *Mississippi Valley Historical Review*, XIII (1926), 365-86.

———, "Spain and the Cherokee Indians, 1783-1798," *North Carolina Historical Review*, IV (1927), 252-69.

Index

Adams, John, 84, 105
Alabama, 71, 137
Amherstburg, Can., 167
Army, United States: inadequate, 32-33, 36, 67; increases, 34, 87; land bounties, 43; need to police frontier, 64-65
Augusta, Treaty of: signed, 27; confirmed, 29; commissioners to investigate, 68, 70; mentioned, 28
Aupaumut, Captain Hendrick, Stockbridge Indian, 92, 156

Beaver, Delaware chief, 156
Benson, Egbert, 179
Beresford, Richard, 175
Blount, William: at Hopewell treaties, 29, 30; governor of Southwest Territory, 71; treaty of Holston, 73; and Cherokee, 77-78; urges firm action, 78, 79; Knox suspicious of, 80; mentioned, 74, 75, 76, 161, 182
Board of Treasury, 34, 179
Boilvin Nicholas, 152
Brant, Joseph: and New York, 17; leads Indians, 31; confederacy, 39,

41; Fort Harmar treaty, 46; organizing resistance, 91; mission for Americans, 92; Maumee council, 94
British, Indian policy, 21, 31, 46, 154, 167, 169, 176
Brownstown, Treaty of, 155
Butler, Richard, 18, 20, 22, 175

Carrington, Edward, 179
Carroll, Daniel, 175, 178
Chase, Jeremiah Townley, 175
Cherokee Indians: and state of Franklin, 25; cede land to Georgia, 27; provoked, 28; Hopewell treaty, 29; Chota Ford treaty, 30; encroached on, 39, 50-51, 56-57, 62, 81, 159; Knox report, 67; Holston treaty, 73-74; civilization of, 74, 83, 112, 128; Philadelphia treaty, 79; Tellico treaties, (1798), 82, 105, (1804), 127, 189, (1805), 127; pressure on, 104, 117, 119, 124, 138-39; agent to, 116; visit Washington, D.C., 118, 140; Washington treaty, 127-28; and Indian removal, 162, 164; men-

Index